Clickers in the Classroom

NEW PEDAGOGIES AND PRACTICES FOR
TEACHING IN HIGHER EDUCATION SERIES

In the same series:

Blended Learning
Across the Disciplines, Across the Academy
Edited by Francine S. Glazer

Cooperative Learning in Higher Education
Across the Disciplines, Across the Academy
Edited by Barbara J. Millis

Just-in-Time Teaching
Across the Disciplines, Across the Academy
Edited by Scott Simkins and Mark H. Maier

Team Teaching
Across the Disciplines, Across the Academy
Edited by Kathryn M. Plank

Using Reflection and Metacognition to Improve Student Learning
Across the Disciplines, Across the Academy
Edited by Matthew Kaplan, Naomi Silver, Danielle LaVaque-Manty, and
Deborah Meizlish

Also in association with James Rhem:

Lesson Study
*Using Classroom Inquiry to Improve Teaching and Learning in Higher
Education*
Bill Cerbin
Foreword by Pat Hutchings

Clickers in the Classroom

Using Classroom Response Systems to Increase Student Learning

Edited by David S. Goldstein and Peter D. Wallis

Foreword by James Rhem

New Pedagogies and Practices for Teaching in Higher Education series

Series Editors: James Rhem and Susan Slesinger

STERLING, VIRGINIA

Sty/us

COPYRIGHT © 2015 BY
STYLUS PUBLISHING, LLC.

Published by Stylus Publishing, LLC
22883 Quicksilver Drive
Sterling, Virginia 20166-2102

Library of Congress Cataloging-in-Publication Data

Clickers in the classroom : using classroom response
systems to increase student learning / edited by David
S. Goldstein and Peter D. Wallis ; foreword by James
Rhem.
pages cm. — (New pedagogies and practices for
teaching in higher education series)
Includes bibliographical references and index.
ISBN 978-1-62036-280-8 (pbk. : alk. paper)
ISBN 978-1-62036-279-2 (cloth : alk. paper)
ISBN 978-1-62036-281-5 (library networkable
e-edition)
ISBN 978-1-62036-282-2 (consumer e-edition)
1. Student response systems. 2. Educational
technology. I. Goldstein, David S., 1962- II. Wallis,
Peter D.
LB1028.3.C625 2015
371.39—dc23

2014047014

13-digit ISBN: 978-1-62036-279-2 (cloth)
13-digit ISBN: 978-1-62036-280-8 (paper)
13-digit ISBN: 978-1-62036-281-5 (library e-edition)
13-digit ISBN: 978-1-62036-282-2 (consumer e-book)

Printed in the United States of America

All first editions printed on acid-free paper
that meets the American National Standards Institute
Z39-48 Standard.

Bulk Purchases

Quantity discounts are available
for use in workshops and for staff
development.
Call 1-800-232-0223

First Edition, 2015

10 9 8 7 6 5 4 3 2 1

Learning anything worthwhile requires patient, formative feedback from people who care. One might say it takes love. Much of my best self has been shaped by my aunts, Joan Gross and Claire Goldstein, and my late uncle, Larry Goldstein. I dedicate my contribution to this volume to them, with love and gratitude.
David S. Goldstein

I echo David's dedication, but add recognition of Lia Grace Wallis. She has always been open, sometimes unsparing, with feedback. She has always sought it, from the world and from me. In the willing sacrifice of her time, she knew me when all my answers were wrong. Love, then and now.
Peter D. Wallis

Contents

Acknowledgments

I am indebted to Dr. James Rhem, who first invited me to produce this volume, and to Susan Schlesinger, who expertly marshaled the book through its development, as well as to the terrific staff of Stylus Publishing. Peter Wallis has been a joy to work with—impressively knowledgeable and unwaveringly reliable. I am also grateful to the innumerable colleagues and students who have taught me so much about teaching and learning. Dr. Bruce Burgett, Dean of the School of Interdisciplinary Arts and Sciences at the University of Washington Bothell, provided a writing retreat at the Whiteley Center, UW Friday Harbor Laboratories, which was invaluable for this project. Thanks, also, to Robyn Smidley for administrative support.

David S. Goldstein
Seattle, Washington

I would like to thank David for being a fantastic collaborator and bringing me into the process of creating this volume. I recognize my adviser, Dr. Virginia Berninger, for her unrelenting dedication to teachers, students, and learning. Particular thanks are due to UW-IT for enabling my growth as an instructional technologist, Jacob Morris for his management, and Phil Reid for his strategic direction. I would also like to thank the innumerable colleagues and coequals who lent their support.

Peter D. Wallis
Seattle, Washington

Foreword

Not that long ago, the word *pedagogy* didn't occur that often in faculty conversations about teaching. Today, one hears it frequently. Without putting too much weight on the prominence of a single word, subtle shifts in discourse, in vocabulary, often do mark significant shifts in thinking, and faculty thinking about teaching has changed over the last several decades. Faculty have always wanted to teach well, wanted their students to learn and succeed, but for a very long time faculty have taught as they were taught; for the students who were like them in temperament and intelligence, the approach worked well enough. When only a highly filtered population of students sought higher education, the need to look beyond those approaches to teaching lay dormant. When a much larger and more diverse population began enrolling, the limits of traditional teaching emerged more sharply.

At the same time, intelligence itself became a more deeply understood phenomenon. Recognition of multiple kinds of intelligence—visual, auditory, kinesthetic, and so on (Gardner, 1983)—found wide acceptance, as did different styles of learning even within those different kinds of intelligence (Myers-Briggs Type Indicator, etc.). Efforts to build ever more effective "thinking machines," that is to say, computers, through artificial intelligence sharpened the understanding of how information needed to be processed in order for it to be assembled and utilized effectively. The seminal article "Cognitive Apprenticeship: Teaching the Craft of Reading, Writing, and Mathematics," by Alan Collins, John Seely Brown, and Susan E. Newman (1989), was one by-product of this research, and one instructive aspect of this work lay in how it looked back to accumulated wisdom to establish its foundations for moving forward. Public schools had long dealt with large, diverse populations rather than highly filtered ones. Teachers there understood *scaffolding, wait time,* and *chunking* in conscious ways that were new to teachers at more advanced levels in education. Now, many of these terms, and more importantly these conscious and deliberate ways of thinking about teaching, have become commonplace in higher education.

Even more recently, all this work has found support and expansion in the findings of neurobiological research into the human brain and how it operates, and in the study of groups and how they operate.

If renewed attention to teaching in higher education began as something of a "fix-it" shop approach aimed at helping individual faculty address teaching problems, it didn't stay that way for long. As Jerry G. Gaff and Ronald D. Simpson (1994) detail in their history of faculty development in the United States, pressure from the burgeoning baby boom population brought the whole business of university teaching up for reconsideration. What was relevant? What were appropriate educational goals, and what were the most effective means of meeting them? Traditionally, the primary expectation of faculty was that they remain current in their fields of expertise. An entirely new set of expectations began to spring up on campuses all over the country.

Change often fails to come easily and smoothly. Generational and social conflicts, together with passionate political conflicts centering on the unpopular war in Vietnam, may have fueled the pressure for changes in teaching while making them more conflict-ridden than they needed to be. But it is important to repeat: Faculty have always wanted to teach well and have their students succeed. As the clouds of conflict from those decades have passed, the intellectual fruits have remained and grown. Some ascribe credit for change in faculty attitudes toward teaching to the social pressures of those decades. Whatever truth lies in that ascription, it seems clear that faculty's innate intellectual curiosity and eagerness to succeed in their life's work deserve equal credit, certainly as they pertain to current faculty interest in improved teaching.

Faculty face a challenge in embracing new understandings of effective teaching not unlike the challenge of any population of diverse intelligences in learning and applying new information. Some of the understandings that emerged in the 1980s (in which much of the new thinking on teaching and learning began to appear) have cross-disciplinary, universal applicability. Such is the case, for example, with the "Seven Principles of Good Practice in Higher Education" developed by Arthur Chickering and Zelda Gamson (1987). But just as diverse people learn in diverse ways, diverse faculty will apply even universal principles in different ways, because both personalities and disciplinary cultures vary. Perhaps that is why many pedagogical insights into effective teaching have not aggregated into one universal, best way to teach. Instead, the forward-moving inquiry into effective teaching has spawned a variety of pedagogical approaches, each with strengths appropriate to particular teaching styles and situations.

Although faculty today have greater curiosity about new understandings of effective ways to teach, they remain as cautious about change as anyone else. If they teach biology, they may wonder how a particular approach that works well in an English literature classroom might play out in a biology course. If they teach English literature, they may wonder if problem-based teaching (an approach highly effective in the sciences) has anything to offer their teaching and if anyone in their discipline has tried it. Every new idea requires translation and receives it in the hands of the next person to take it up and apply it in his or her work. And this is as it should be. Thus, this series of books strives to give faculty examples of new approaches to teaching as they are being applied in a representative sample of academic disciplines. From the start, the central goal of the National Teaching and Learning Forum has been to offer faculty ideas in contexts, that is to say, to present enough theory so that ideas about teaching and learning make sense intellectually, but then to present those ideas in applied contexts. From this combination, faculty can see how an approach might fit into their own practice. Faculty do not need formulae; they need only to see ideas in contexts. They'll take it from there. And so our series of books offers faculty a multipaned window into a variety of nontraditional pedagogical approaches now being applied with success in different disciplines in higher education. Faculty will look in and find something of value for their own teaching. As I've said and believe with all my heart, faculty have always wanted to teach well and see their students succeed.

This addition to the series pushes active understanding of the teaching and learning dynamic one important step further. For some time, faculty have struggled with the pressure to adopt all sorts of new technology into their teaching. White boards have replaced blackboards; PowerPoint has become de rigueur. Again, it's been a struggle, and not everyone has welcomed it. But one bit of technology is proving a wonderful tool that fits nicely with the growing findings about student engagement and human learning: the classroom response system, commonly called the "clicker." Today's students grew up with remote controls in their hands. They're comfortable with a certain level of control. When they discover that a clicker in their hand opens up an entirely new level of active participation and discovery in the classroom, they feel engaged in a mode they already know, and robust learning takes off in new ways that are appropriate to their generation and the technology that's now part of all our lives. The examples of successful clicker use David S. Goldstein and Peter D. Wallis have gathered for this volume will help faculty see how to adopt clickers into their teaching and, with the click of a few buttons, see their students' learning take off.

—James Rhem,
Executive Editor,
The National Teaching & Learning Forum

REFERENCES

Chickering, A. W., & Gamson, Z. F. (1987). Seven principles for good practice in undergraduate education. *AAHE Bulletin, 3,* 2–6.

Collins, A., Brown, J. S., & Newman, S. E. (1989). Cognitive apprenticeship: Teaching the craft of reading, writing and mathematics. In L. B. Resnick (Ed.), *Knowing, learning and instruction: Essays in honor of Robert Glaser* (pp. 453–494). Hillsdale, NJ: Erlbaum.

Gaff, J. G., & Simpson, R. D. (1994). Faculty development in the United States. *Innovative Higher Education, 18*(3), 167–176.

Gardner, H. (1983). *Frames of mind: The theory of multiple intelligences.* New York, NY: Basic Books.

Preface

Passive learning is dead. The final nail in the coffin has been driven home by Scott Freeman and his colleagues in their recent, blockbuster meta-analysis of active learning (i.e., learning in which students have to do something rather than simply listen to lectures and absorb written text). Freeman and colleagues (2014) analyzed 225 peer-reviewed, empirical articles that compared an intervention group that engaged with active learning with a control group of students exposed to conventional, passive approaches in science and mathematics courses. Starting with a null hypothesis that passive learning works best, the researchers found overwhelmingly that they must reject the null hypothesis. Specifically, here is what they found (Bhatia, 2014):

- "Students in traditional lecture courses are 1.5 times more likely to fail, compared to students in courses with active learning" (para. 9).
- "Students in active learning classes outperform those in traditional lectures on identical exams" (para. 12).
- "There is a growing body of evidence showing that active learning differentially benefits students of color and/or students from disadvantaged backgrounds and/or women in male-dominated fields. It's not a stretch to claim that lecturing actively discriminates against underrepresented students" (para. 16).

Students in active learning classrooms also outperformed those in classes taught by celebrated lecturers; that is, active learning trumps even brilliant lectures in terms of student learning outcomes.

How, then, shall teachers "activate" their classes?

The literature is rife with active learning approaches that improve learning. Naturally, some techniques are more labor- and time-intensive than others. One relatively easy yet effective means for engaging students in active learning is the use of clickers.

When used well, classroom response systems (or CRSs, also known as student response systems, individual response systems, or, informally, clickers) improve student learning outcomes in several ways (Goldstein, 2013): They elicit discussion contributions from otherwise reticent students and enhance collaboration, even in large lecture courses (Klein, 2009); they foster more honest responses to discussion prompts (Bruff, 2010); they increase students' engagement and satisfaction with the classroom environment (Fredericksen & Ames, 2009); and they provide an instantaneous method of formative assessment (Briggs & Keyek-Franssen, 2010), all of which are associated with best practices in learning. Many faculty members, however, might be hesitant to try this potentially enriching technique without firsthand accounts of success or detailed examples of implementation. This book provides teachers with several ideas and suggestions that would be quickly applicable in their own classes.

Like all pedagogical interventions, CRSs are no panacea, and the authors included in this volume candidly describe some avoidable and some inevitable pitfalls. When used thoughtfully, however, clickers can deepen student learning by increasing student engagement and providing formative, instantaneous feedback to the instructor, who can make adjustments to a class meeting on the fly to better address student understandings or misunderstandings.

Many articles have been published in teaching-related and disciplinary journals regarding the use of CRSs. Derek Bruff's book *Teaching With Classroom Response Systems* (2009) provided a solid theoretical foundation and limited case studies in various disciplines, but it is already five years old and therefore does not represent the latest theoretical and empirical scholarship in the field, and it does not provide sustained case studies from a broad spectrum of disciplines, as we do in this volume. The chapters assembled here represent all major divisions of disciplines, from the humanities to STEM fields; moreover, they address the use of clickers in research methodology courses; in professional, career-oriented courses such as hospitality studies; and in peer tutor training programs. The authors and examples come from all kinds of higher education institutions and from all regions of the country. The volume therefore presents a comprehensive, practical, teacher-to-teacher overview of clicker usage throughout higher education.

We begin this volume with a comprehensive history of the development of CRSs and a survey of empirical research to provide a context for current best practices, and then present nine chapters providing authentic, effective uses of clickers in all types of academic disciplines, elaborating on the ways that CRSs can, for example, enable students of diverse backgrounds and personalities to contribute to classroom learning; elicit instant feedback from students regarding their understanding of the material and/or their thoughts or attitudes, so the teacher can respond immediately; and obtain honest responses to sensitive questions that cannot be effectively answered with a show of hands. Each of these chapters highlights a different discipline, and they are written by distinguished teachers with successful experience using CRSs in their courses. These chapters include suggestions for similar uses and, because the book's purpose is to share ideas rather than proselytize, also share limitations and caveats. The tone is intended to be conversational, teacher to teacher: candid, engaging, and jargon free. We also provide an annotated list of further resources, such as books, articles, and videos.

Because CRSs are increasingly popular in community colleges and four-year colleges and universities, and because the examples are drawn from a variety of classroom contexts and academic disciplines, this book is intended to appeal to a broad audience in higher education, including present and aspiring faculty members, academic support services professionals, and faculty development experts. We hope you find the ideas herein to be helpful in your own teaching.

REFERENCES

Bhatia, A. (2014). Active learning leads to higher grades and fewer failing students in science, math, and engineering. *Wired*. Retrieved November 2, 2014, from http://wired.com/2014/05/empzeal-active-learning/

Briggs, C., & Keyek-Franssen, D. (2010, January). CATs with clickers: Using learner response systems for formative assessments in the classroom. Presented at the 2010 EDUCAUSE Learning Initiative Conference, Austin, TX. Retrieved November 2, 2014, from EDUCAUSE at http://www.educause.edu/eli/events/eli-annual-meeting/2010/cats-clickers-using-learner-response-systems-formative-assessments-classroom-innovative-pr

Bruff, D. (2009). *Teaching with classroom response systems: Creating active learning environments*. San Francisco, CA: Jossey-Bass.

Bruff, D. (2010). Multiple-choice questions you wouldn't put on a test: Promoting deep learning using clickers. *Essays on Teaching Excellence, 21*(3).

Fredericksen, E. E., & Ames, M. (2009). Can a $30 piece of plastic improve learning? An evaluation of personal response systems in large classroom settings. SIGCHI Conference Paper. Accessed November 2, 2014, from EDUCAUSE at http://net.educause.edu/ir/library/pdf/csd2690.pdf

Freeman, S., Eddy, S. L., McDonough, M., Smith, M. K., Okaroafor, N., Jordt, H., & Wenderoth, M. P. (2014). Active learning increases student performance in science, engineering, and mathematics. *Proceedings of the National Academy of Sciences, 111,* 8410–8415. Retrieved August 4, 2014, from http://www.pnas.org/content/111/23/8410.full.pdf+html

Goldstein, D. S. (2013). What are they thinking? Best practices for classroom response systems ("clickers"). *National Teaching & Learning Forum, 22,* 5–6.

Klein, K. (2009). Promoting collaborative social learning communities with student response systems. *Journal of Online Learning and Teaching, 5*(4). Retrieved from http://jolt.merlot.org/vol5no4/klein_1209.htm

What's Constant?

Clickers Across Contexts

Peter D. Wallis

The norms established in the classroom have strong effects on students' achievement. In some schools, the norms could be expressed as "don't get caught not knowing something." Others encourage academic risk taking and opportunities to make mistakes, obtain feedback, and revise. Clearly, if students are to reveal their preconceptions, questions, and progress toward understanding the subject matter, the norms of the school must support their doing so (National Research Council, 2000).

Students are not the only ones afraid of being caught not knowing something. As an instructional technologist, I am deeply aware of the pace of change in technologies for learning and the difficulties these changes can create for faculty. Today's technological changes can go as far as updating a web-based learning management system (LMS) in the space between one class and the next, leaving faculty unsure of where to click. As a student of the learning sciences, however, I look for what remains constant in learning—how brains learn across time, across cultural contexts, and across spaces. Together, these two areas of study—the rapid change of technology and the relative constancy of the brain—are forming helpful models that can guide the way teachers innovate in their teaching and the way rapidly changing technology is developed and applied.

Five days a week, I work with university teachers to apply technology in teaching and learning. Despite the belief that university-level teachers and curricula stay constant from year to year, many of these teachers are eager to adopt new models and new tools (Beyer, Taylor, & Gillmore, 2013). Interacting with faculty has provided me with a wealth of stories and examples about the use of classroom response systems (CRSs) and other technologies, in and out of the classroom. This work has also driven me to understand the human brain and its relative constancy in the face of rapid educational and technological change. We still have much to discover about the human brain, but what we have discovered so far can inform how we adopt technology today.

To be clear: teachers are not the only ones challenged by the pace of technological change. Students have commented personally, and in our research, that their busy lives often leave insufficient time to keep up with the latest and greatest technologies. Sometimes their instructors adopt these technologies because they believe students expect them to have the latest and greatest. Faculty can be surprised to find that students also struggle to adapt to technological changes in teaching and learning (Giacomini et al., 2011; Giacomini et al., 2013). It therefore falls to teachers to justify their use of technology beyond wanting to offer the "newest." This also reminds us of the value of adopting relatively simple technologies, for the sake of students as well as faculty.

While keeping the technology simple is a benefit, faculty stories of successes and failures consistently bring home the need for a sound, high-level understanding of learning. Faculty members who teach effectively with technology understand, sometimes implicitly, but more often explicitly, how effective learning happens. They think about and sometimes even conduct research on how students learn, and they apply those thoughts to their teaching. The contributors to this book argue that classroom response technologies have been effective in teaching and learning. In fact, a recent, comprehensive literature review found classroom response technologies to be effective teaching and learning tools (Kay & LeSage, 2009). Discussing, theoretically, why classroom response technologies have been effective can help to reveal how instructors or developers looking to adopt or enhance CRSs can optimize their effectiveness.

There is an additional benefit to understanding the learning sciences perspective in this book. In understanding the background, readers will be able to connect examples throughout this book with the theoretical frameworks given here. As the concepts make sense, the stories will as well. Readers will be able to construct helpful criticism as they think through uses of technologies. Classroom response technologies, like all teaching technologies, are tools, not panaceas. They need to be applied intelligently to be effective. Students' reactions to classroom response technologies are highly dependent on the ways in which faculty use them. They are pleased with faculty who use systems to give feedback and promote discussion and displeased with uses that merely track attendance (Kay & LeSage, 2009; Guthrie & Carlin, 2004). Beyond current use, technologies will continue to change. Mobile phones, LMS integrations, and new forms of asynchronous presentation may be on the verge of changing how classroom response is used or implemented. This chapter, and this book, can give readers a good starting point as they manage and grow with those changes. Lessons learned about learning from classroom response can be applied outside of the classroom, to LMS-based interactions, to embedded-video quizzing, and across broader contexts.

The pace of change in the human brain is slow compared to the pace of technology. Although the individual brain has been shown to be wonderfully malleable even in adulthood (a concept broadly called "neuroplasticity"), our general brain systems have distinct commonalities that enable our interactions as learners with classroom response technologies. Many things are still unclear about how exactly the physical brain learns, but the coordination of psychology, educational psychology, cognitive science, and neuroscience has started to shed light on the general processes that operate while we learn. We can even begin to pick out the processes by which specific technologies, like those involved in classroom response, work in the learning brain.

Classroom response technologies work through a combination of executive attention, social engagement, and rapid, meaningful feedback. The first thing that effective use of classroom response technologies does is to bring learners' executive networks to attention by engaging them in a decision. This involvement calls upon both short- and long-term memory to try to create or recall an answer. Attention does not function alone. When we give an answer, we learn from feedback, not just from presentation. Action followed by correction is a deeply useful way of learning across a number of technologies, and can be particularly active in classroom response technologies, especially in larger groups. Finally, innovative uses of clickers can drive social engagement, scaffolding students into the habits of group work. Operating together, these basic lessons in educational psychology can help us think through cases of clicker use, and toward new uses of classroom response technologies as the technologies grow.

These basic lessons in educational psychology also point to classroom response's role as one of a number of "active learning" techniques. Recent research has shown unambiguously that active learning is more effective than traditional lecture (Freeman et al., 2014) in science and mathematics courses. This research includes a number of examples from classroom-response-based interventions. A long history of active learning, stretching back through medieval and late Roman teachers to a Greek ancestry, challenges the "traditional" in traditional lecture. Active learning has a long and storied history of involving students' executive attention, giving them feedback, and engaging them in a social context. The cultural context and the educational content of the pursuit may differ, but the aim of the pursuit—learning—remains steady in our changing brains.

Exciting research is ongoing. Scientists are discovering more and more about how brains learn, and they use technology to do so. New research gradually uncovers the mysteries of the human brain, while the technology advances like a sprint. Understanding how people learn can help designers, technologists, and the developers and innovators who make the technologies bring additional value to learning. Together, we can work toward predicting when things will go wrong and repairing them when they do. We can adapt to new technologies and encourage designers to make more effective technologies for teaching and learning. We cannot do these things without a goal or a path. To build learning machines, we need to understand how we learn. We can teach and learn better, but first we must learn *how*.

ATTENTION

Like the entertainment industry, education has always sought to get attention. CRSs, too, are deeply involved with attention—most obviously, attention to the current discussion and to the memory of past discussions. As such, it should be relatively unsurprising that one story of the origin of CRSs is set in Hollywood.

As the story goes, around 1966, the Audience Studies Institute created the earliest forms of audience response systems, which gave rise to CRSs (Broderick, 2009; Collins, 2008; Edlund, Gustafson, Heldner, & Hjalmarsson, 2008; Elias & Esswein, 2012; Vane & Gross, 1994). In the earliest cases, these systems were a simple knob wired into theater seat armrests. Twisted all the way to the right, this knob indicated great enjoyment. Twisted all the way to the left, the knob indicated boredom or displeasure. Major television and film studios paid the Audience Response Institute to measure responses to their films, which gave them feedback on the level of attention potential customers were paying to their products and the level of enjoyment in a half- or two-hour block of entertainment.

Significant research has shown that, besides intuition and years of experience, attention is vital to learning (Jensen, 2008; Kruschke, 2003; Medina, 2008; National Research Council, 2000; Sousa, 2012). Attention is something we should seek in education, as in entertainment. Other educational technologies have clearer relationships with entertainment. Video-based education, which began with television and has more recently spread to YouTube and other video-hosting sites, and game-based education have looked to entertainment industries for models of attracting and maintaining attention. There are differences, however, between the ways a CRS engages or involves students' attention and the ways a video may do so.

Neuroscience of Attention

Michael Posner, professor emeritus of psychology at the University of Oregon, has been studying attention for most of his career. In research that contributed to his winning a National Medal of Science, Posner and his colleagues applied both "subtractive methods" and neuroimaging (measuring activation in the brain) to study attention, memory, and other cognitive functions. Posner and colleagues' two theoretical stances—subtractive, in which mental skills are made up of other, smaller mental skills, and functional localization, meaning that particular areas of the brain specialize in certain skills—contributed tremendously to the study of attention. In their framework, Posner and colleagues found that there is an "alerting" system that tells individuals there are things they should pay attention to, and that this system is both physically and functionally different from the "orienting" and "executive" networks. The executive network is specifically involved in guiding attention consciously (Petersen & Posner, 2012; Posner, 1980; Posner, 2012). One particularly interesting finding is that even the executive function may be split—into systems that maintain attention on a single set of tasks and systems that support switching back and forth between contexts (Petersen & Posner, 2012).

What does this have to do with CRSs? Put simply, systems that get attention can get different "parts" of attention. A television show might get one's attention in terms of the alerting and orienting systems, but leave out the executive networks. The popular phrase "I couldn't tear my eyes away" represents this phenomenon quite well. Leaving out this "attentional spotlight" (a phrase John Medina [2008] likes to use) reduces the engagement of decision making and working memory systems. Students who practice executive attention in class not only attend better to the material, but also practice manipulating and retrieving ideas and concepts from the class in their working memory.

Getting Executive Attention

In an alternative story of the genesis of classroom response, an IBM researcher and futurist named William Simmons invented audience response. This story is better supported than that of the Audience Response Institute (Simmons & Elsberry, 1988). Simmons noticed that meetings were often long and boring and involved a fair bit of discussion on points everyone agreed upon. Simmons was not the first to notice boring meetings, but he thought he could do something about them. Simmons, then, invented a dial-based machine he called the "Consensor" by which people would "dial in" their consensus or agreement on a point, and the meeting would focus on the points upon which participants disagreed.

This origin story bears more resemblance to the value of classroom response: engaging executive, decision-making attention on points of disagreement. This difference raises an important point when it comes to attention as researched by Posner. Students or teachers can pay attention while actually doing little to engage executive networks. In fact, engaging the executive decision-making network, that is, asking oneself, "Am I enjoying this enough to twist the dial to the right?," may interfere with the sort of deep, immersive attention that films and television shows seek to elicit. Consequently, the technology hypothetically used by the Audience Studies Institute could consistently be expected to bias the results of their measures of attention simply by changing the type of attention paid.

Example: Engaging Executive Attention With Environmental Media

At the University of Washington's Seattle campus, Lekelia Jenkins teaches in the School of Marine and Environmental Affairs. In her classrooms, she elicits students' executive attention in a way reminiscent of the work done by the Audience Studies Institute and IBM. Jenkins is charged with not only helping her students understand and remember many things about marine life, but also engaging them in thinking critically about that marine life and how our choices as individuals and as a society influence it. To this end, she has developed a unique method of using CRSs in her own teaching.

Jenkins engages students in thinking through media they already encounter in their everyday lives. She has students in class watch two-to-five-minute videos of public service announcements from organizations that seek to do science education yet often have a political agenda. Her choice of media alone sparks students' attention, because students recognize the impact and meaning of the source. It helps that the videos are, in one way or another, entertaining or emotionally engaging. While the students watch these videos, they are charged with rating them using Turning Technologies' handheld transmitters (clickers). As the video plays, students click responses on a scale from 1, for "pure rhetoric," to 5, for "pure scientific evidence."

When the video finishes, Jenkins uses the Turning Technologies software to display a chart of students' real-time reactions, from the first to the last minute of the viewing. This chart sparks almost immediate discussion and allows the class to go back and review points where there were high levels of rhetoric or of scientific evidence. Students then discuss what features of the video led them to make that assessment and the benefits and potential drawbacks of presenting information in this way. By the end of class, they have refined their ability to distinguish rhetoric from scientific evidence. Students come to realize that rhetoric is important and useful in engaging audiences and crafting poignant, lasting messages, but that ideas need to be supported with objective evidence. Students are then equipped to not only consume mass media critically but also to use rhetoric appropriately when crafting scientific messages.

In contrast with entertainment, education often seeks to train minds not for passive attention, but for executive engagement and judgment. Jenkins's practice of teaching her students to judge the moment-by-moment scientific accuracy of environmental advertisements often runs counter to the original purpose of those advertisements—to wrap viewers up in a wave of emotion that overrides their executive judgment. Likewise, at IBM, Simmons was not seeking to create receptive executives who would accept any and all reasons, excuses, or explanations. Jenkins and Simmons sought to engage not only passive and emotional networks, but also executive networks and executive attention, which are involved in evaluation and critical judgment, comparisons with past experience, and testing for the cohesiveness of any explanation or chain of reasoning.

A cluster of skills enables Jenkins's use of CRSs. She thereby provides an excellent example of technology adoption by a faculty member. She does not claim to be highly technology savvy, but when exploring CRSs for the first time during an hour-long workshop, she quickly hunted for functionality that made sense to her in the context of her teaching, and focused on using that functionality. This allowed her to learn one piece of a complicated system very well and use it particularly well in class. This focus allows Jenkins to adapt to technological changes in devices at a measured and thoughtful pace, because she does not need to rethink her device use every time one thing changes, but only when those changes have an impact on her own use of CRSs. Jenkins is therefore able to build and manipulate the structure of her class around the discussions the students are having, integrating their thoughts and discussions into the conversation. Executive engagement with CRSs does not exist in isolation; it interacts with other skills and values in Jenkins's teaching.

Students have responded well to her engagement of their executive attention. They have consistently given positive feedback—in person, in course reviews, and by recommending her course to other students. These results are not unique. Other studies, including internal studies by the University of Washington's Information Technology department (UW-IT) and those by Guthrie and Carlin (2004) and Kay and LeSage (2009), have found significant student satisfaction with CRSs.

Broader Concerns

Students' satisfaction with CRSs, of course, interacts with other parts of the history and context of classroom response, including price and technological growth. CRSs were not tested at universities until the latter half of the 1990s, and even then, they were tested in classes of fewer than 20 students due to cost and technology limitations. It is questionable whether students would be pleased with audience response systems if each clicker cost as much as a 1996 Macintosh computer. It has taken only about 20 years to go from little evidence and small classes to more than 70 peer-reviewed studies of classroom response, and some courses enrolling more than 2,000 students engaged in classroom response. Given the near ubiquity of cell phones and wireless technology, I am excited for what the next 20 years will bring, but the value-to-price ratio for students must remain high enough to make this possible.

The effectiveness of CRSs in drawing attention, especially to points of difference, raises an important question. If students respond with (and therefore focus on) their differences (on questions where, necessarily, this means some students must answer incorrectly), will they recite, and therefore remember, their errors? Isn't the role of the teacher to get the students to remember what is correct? Research in another educational technology that more clearly shares a history with entertainment—video—can help elucidate this point.

FEEDBACK

Derek Muller is a successful YouTube educator. He runs a large enough YouTube channel (Veritasium) to be paid to teach people about something he loves: physics. While Muller's wonder at the surprising order of the world is apparent in his videos, he uses his doctoral work to make these videos uniquely educational. Muller's doctoral dissertation in physics education from the University of Sydney was based on his experiments in which students were either shown a traditional lecture or forced to make predictions about the outcome of events, and were then shown the outcome and an explanation through traditional lecture. Students who were forced to make predictions reported leaving more confused, but they subsequently performed substantially better and came to appreciate this active, engaged form of teaching (Muller, 2008).

The Importance of Feedback

Muller's work confirmed previous research, which had not been applied to video-based education. Raymond Kulhavy (1977) found in evaluating writing feedback that students who formulate answers before they receive feedback will learn more than students who do not. These findings contrast with the traditional idea that students should first learn and then receive feedback on what they did or did not retain. Muller and Kulhavy independently suggested that, instead, students should not have questions answered before the questions emerge for them out of their own curiosity. This incitement of curiosity has a long history in educational philosophy, both in John Dewey's hypotheses (Dewey, 1916/1997) and the work of Frase, Patrick, and Schumer (1970), who confirmed, partially empirically, that students who were asked questions more often learned more than those who were asked fewer questions. Will Thalheimer (2003) likewise found that simply inciting students to mentally answer questions and formulate those questions for themselves led to more learning. Muller's work extends this line of thinking in ways that make it more applicable to our changing, technologically altered university education today.

Of course, not all feedback is the same. Feedback given at the end of a course or section, judging a student's performance (often called "summative" feedback), differs from feedback given in the midst of the course, while students still have the chance to use that feedback to change their understanding ("formative" feedback). CRSs are particularly effective as technologies for formative feedback, and formative feedback is particularly effective in teaching and learning. Ironically, CRSs are particularly effective in formative feedback in part because of their technological limitations: They are rarely secure or consistent enough to deliver a large segment of the students' grades. Likewise, Bangert-Drowns, Kulik, Kulik, and Morgan (1991) warned that the effects of feedback, especially in testing situations, can vary widely, and can, at times, result in negative treatment effects. They highlight the need for specificity in feedback and the need for students to be receptive to it.

Jason Moser and colleagues (2011) have begun to build an empirical understanding of how the anxiety that comes with potentially being wrong results in increased or decreased learning. They focused particularly on students who maintained a "growth mindset," that is, believed that intelligence was not fixed but instead that their efforts would result in increased skill. In studying the electrical responses of the brain, Moser and colleagues found that students with a growth mindset paid more attention to their mistakes and had increased accuracy following those mistakes and correction. Moreover, they found that even the timing of the brains' electrical responses differed between students with a growth mindset and those who believed that intelligence is fixed.

These findings align with those of Kornell, Hays, and Bjork (2009), who found that even if students simply could not remember an answer when prompted for it, they were more likely to learn the answer than students who simply presented with the answer twice. This finding suggests that students who have never heard the right answer to a question are still learning when they hear it, and the finding should encourage teachers to present challenging questions in classroom response, especially if they keep the grade impact of these questions low. Moser and colleagues' later research found that long-term anxiety (about grades and difficult questions, for example) negatively affected performance (Moser, Moran, Schroder, Donnellan, & Yeung, 2013).

Feedback at Several Difficulty Levels: Ohio State University

The Physics Education Group at Ohio State University has focused its research on the difficulty of classroom response questions. They have created and studied several interesting models of question grouping. In the primary method, students are first asked an easy question to instill confidence and make early participation rewarding and then asked a hard question to make sure the concept was understood and to engender discussion. Following the first hard question and discussion, students are asked a second difficult question, usually involving the transfer of the concept to a superficially new situation. After extensive testing, the Ohio State University group has found these question groups to be significantly more effective than single questions (Ding, Reay, Lee, & Bao, 2008; Reay, Bao, Warnakulasooriya, & Baugh, 2006; Reay, Li, & Bao, 2008). The Ohio State University group is also testing rapid-fire, medium-difficulty sets of questions that span several different situations (Beatty & Gerace, 2009).

In his well-publicized book on expertise, K. A. Ericsson (2006) identified getting things wrong and attending to specific feedback as key elements of the "deliberate practice" through which all the experts his team studies attain their high performance goals. Feedback is deeply important, because it allows us to change our practice. Without feedback and subsequent evaluation of our answers or behaviors, those answers or behaviors are very unlikely to change. Ericsson's model, along with the other feedback models discussed, lend credence to the Ohio State University findings, as students are both developing a network of understanding and getting more specific feedback as several questions are presented, which encourages and enables them to home in on where their misunderstandings lie.

Examples of Feedback: Historical and Present

Given the value of feedback to learning, it should come as no surprise that feedback has been incorporated into meaningful pedagogical practices throughout educational history. The popular medieval educator, philosopher, and logician Peter Abelard based his teaching on the open debate of all points, with the whole class empowered to give feedback on the factual or logical correctness of any argument (Saettler, 1967). This practice placed him in deep opposition to better-known practices of copying and rote memorization. Likewise, Socrates's particular attention to feedback on students' logical reasoning has had an incalculable impact on his place in educational history. More recently, behaviorist psychologists like B. F. Skinner have strongly emphasized the feedback received by organisms from the environment (Saettler, 1967).

This discussion provides only a brief outline of a few historical perspectives on the role of feedback in learning and on how these historical perspectives apply to one technology. Given the broad history and key importance of feedback in the learning process, it is vital to state that CRSs provide only one type of feedback. Although students can extract feedback on a mental heuristic, concept, or fact, CRSs are, for the instructor, a way of giving feedback to a whole class, not to an individual. The individual benefit is always involved with a professor's own negotiation with and understanding of the class, and the individual students' ability to analyze and recognize their own errors.

Feedback that helps students understand their misconceptions is of primary concern to one UW faculty member, Daryl Pedigo. In his introductory physics courses at UW, Pedigo teaches many students who are majoring not in physics but in engineering or other sciences. In a recent conversation, Pedigo stated:

> If you are just watching the world, it's pretty much Aristotelian. Things don't move by themselves. It's pretty hard to develop a mathematical model of that world. Newton's big insight was that objects—a lot of objects—are "normally" in motion, and stay in motion unless acted upon by an outside force.
>
> If we had all grown up living on a spaceship between the stars, the natural state would be moving through space at a constant speed. That's the big difference. People come in with an Aristotelian view, and it's hard for them to change those views. Students don't usually struggle with the math; it's the filtering of the concepts that are wrong, or that don't apply.

Physics can be an unintuitive subject, as the assumptions and predications we are used to making about the physical world can break down in surprising and important ways. Because of this, students can assume that they correctly interpret or understand a law of motion when they do not. Daryl uses questions that test understanding of the concepts involved, so that the students get the feedback they need in order to improve in time for that improvement to be meaningful.

Pedigo's use of audience response systems is similar to the uses of the Mazur Group at Harvard University: Both focus on the understanding of concepts rather than blank retention of particular facts or definitions. Both Pedigo and the Mazur Group focus on CRSs as formative, rather than summative, assessment, using the systems to give students needed feedback on their understanding before those students have to respond on a test, with all of an exam's stresses and finality. Their practices differ, however, in that Pedigo spends less time on peer tutoring, a specialty of Mazur's lab (Crouch & Mazur, 2001), and focuses follow-up questions on students' ability to transfer a concept to a situation that sounds superficially different. This transfer is evidence that they understand the underlying physics (e.g., laws of motion), rather than only the surface features (e.g., what objects are acted upon).

Pedigo also uses the feedback gathered to adjust his teaching, covering a subject in less depth if the class understands it well. Here again, CRSs interact with a total context: Students who struggle with a concept that does not challenge the rest of the class can refer to the lecture notes Pedigo posts to the course website or to short topic videos provided by an outside company.

Finally, Pedigo advocates teaching with classroom response technology and believes in its value for faculty interested in teaching with these systems. In addition to evaluating existing solutions, he works with other teachers in the Physics Department to acquaint them with Hyper-Interactive Teaching Technology (H-ITT), a CRS product he uses. The Physics Department maintains this system because it is fast and easy for busy faculty to adopt quickly, making engagement with active learning more effective and widespread within the department.

Neuroscience of Feedback

In order to better understand empirically why reviewing errors and feedback on errors can be so helpful in educating brains (even more helpful, perhaps, than novelty), one must understand a bit about how memory works. Unfortunately, what little we understand about human memory is partially summed up in the phrase "neurons that fire together, wire together." Neurons are tiny cells in our brains, most of which collect "votes" from other neurons and pass those votes along by way of an electrical action potential that sparks off chemical signals from the neuron's own axon terminal. These chemical signals then count as votes in other neurons. Furthermore, the neurons can "grow" branches toward sources of votes and become more receptive to those votes (Diamond & Hopson, 1999; Engert & Bonhoeffer, 1999; Fischer, Kaech, Knutti, & Matus, 1998). The adjustment of neurons to the feedback around them is termed *long-term potentiation* and is a key part of memory throughout the brain. At a micro-level, our thoughts can be understood as polling machines.

"Firing," however, is not always positive. Neuron firing can also *inhibit* a network from firing. In such cases, if an error is detected, the network of thoughts and associations that makes that error can be inhibited, and this inhibition can strengthen positive associations with the correct answer (Markman, 2012). In addition, these networks can only be created in connection with pre-existing networks. To simplify, the more well-connected a network is, the stronger it tends to be. The more effectively we can help students to construct long-term conceptual networks of activation and inhibition, the more effectively they will learn. As such, giving students the opportunity for social interaction can strengthen their learning, promoting thought by speaking and social interaction as well as by writing and hearing, engaging all these networks in understanding and remembering a concept.

GROUP ENGAGEMENT

Although a lack of individual-level feedback can be a drawback of CRSs, group learning and peer tutoring have helped some groups and disciplines to turn this drawback into a benefit. At Harvard University, the Mazur Group focuses on peer tutoring in physics, utilizing CRSs for "ConcepTests," which engage their students by asking them to explain the fundamental concepts with which they are dealing. These ConcepTest peer discussions are sparked when 30% to 80% of students answer differently from each other. If less than 30% answer correctly, the concept is reviewed, and if more than 80% answer correctly, the top remaining misconception is briefly explained by lecture (Lasry, 2008). In the peer discussion, often called peer instruction, students spend two to three minutes trying to convince each other that their position is correct. This helps them to externalize their thinking so that they can get meaningful feedback on it, a vital part of learning that encourages transfer and metacognition (National Research Council, 2000). (A number of the Mazur Group's ConcepTests are freely available at www.deas .harvard.edu/ilt.)[1]

In my experience at the University of Washington, the Biology Education Research Group (BERG, http://uwberg.com) is particularly successful in its efforts to apply peer-to-peer discussion in class. Several BERG faculty and graduate students were the authors of the active-learning meta-analysis discussed earlier (Freeman et al., 2014). In addition to applying ConcepTest-style discussions to their learning, UW Biology students are sometimes asked to come to a group consensus and respond to the classroom response questions as a group rather than as individuals. This integrates vitally different ways of thinking into classroom response, as students must work with consensus and with group agreement in order to achieve a group answer. The need for a uniform response from the group puts something at stake in the discussions.

I have discussed with BERG's Ben Wiggins his ongoing research on students' engagement with CRSs and with each other. Having well-planned active learning exercises helped Wiggins step in when another teacher's accident left Wiggins with a sudden additional load of more than 1,000 students for half of a quarter. In ongoing research, Wiggins is beginning to turn the methods of biology back on biology teaching: Measuring students' biological activity cycles during active and passive learning, Wiggins has found that students who are required to be responsive are far more active by biological measures than students who are only asked to listen, especially after the first 10 minutes. This likely will come as no surprise to anyone who regularly speaks to large groups. In addition, BERG is now beginning to engage students with connections to their lives outside of class. Students are aggregating their own self-documented sleep records to a class data set and using technological tools to analyze the spread of circadian rhythms.

Sociocultural Learning and Vygotsky

The Soviet psychologist Lev Vygotsky has been particularly influential regarding the integration of different contexts of learning (peer, personal experience, cases). In the early 20th century, Vygotsky helped clarify how human social interactions use feedback to influence the range of individual knowledge, and guide learners as they develop. He is best known for the concept of a "zone of proximal development," the part of a new skill a learner can do only with help. This basic idea—that some skills are "close enough" (proximal) to be grasped with help—has shed light on learning in and out of school, from how children learn about the moon to how undergraduates learn the physics of rocket science (Wallace, 2009). It is important to note that action in this zone of proximal development will generally incite errors because it stretches students' skills. Vygotsky has had a decisive influence among educational thinkers since the 1970s, though his ideas have not permeated popular culture as much as, say, Skinner's.

Vygotsky's basic insight into the interaction between the social context and the learner is simple at its heart, but profound in its application. The idea that students are driven by what they already know, what those around them know, and their direct context is both a helpful framework for considering current technologies and learning contexts and a helpful rebuttal of both Socratic (students learn through debate with a lone, wise teacher) and Skinnerian (students learn through the reinforcement of their context) models. Vygostky helps make the nature of the necessary feedback clear: Feedback needs to be built upon what learners already know and upon the resources they have around them, so that they can practice skills within their zone of proximal development. CRSs, when used well, provide the opportunity for learners to do just this; the more knowledgeable teacher can give feedback appropriate to the context of the developing learner. CRSs do this by allowing the teacher to gather feedback on what the students know, give students feedback on understanding what they do (and do not) understand, and prompt students to use each other as resources. All of this feedback occurs in a larger social context, within which students are gaining new skills and vocabulary in response to the resources and networks in which they are asked to participate.

Low-Tech Options for Socially Engaging Audience Response

Social engagement drives some of the most well-known uses of classroom response. Earlier in this chapter, we discussed Lekelia Jenkins's use of classroom response to drive student discussion. Likewise, groups in physics and biology use classroom response to drive student discussion of the vital concepts in their fields. Technology need not be a limiting factor in creating meaningful peer interaction. While digital CRSs offer the strong benefits of creating records and allowing later analysis of gathered data, anyone looking to get started easily without crossing the technological barriers can, for example, create "flash cards" for their students to use. These are simply differently colored cards handed out to all students. Instead of selecting A, B, C, or D, students hold up a colored card to indicate a particular response. For questions for which there is a need for anonymity, where students might be embarrassed to show that they do not know the correct answer to the class, or a particularly sensitive subject is discussed, each card can be handed off to another student three times in a scramble, so that there are three levels of remove between the cardholder and his or her card. The students, then, do not hold up their own answer card, but the anonymized answer card of someone else in the group (Lasry, 2008).

Public Errors, Anonymity, and Growth Mindset

Just like classroom response, social engagement and peer tutoring can be used well or poorly in teaching and learning. Many students report appreciating the anonymity of CRSs (Guthrie & Carlin, 2004; Kay & LeSage, 2009). Several sources note that, in particular, students with a fixed-intelligence rather than a growth mindset, as well as students coming from cultures where intelligence is treated as fixed and where it is important not to reveal your ignorance, value the anonymity of CRSs. These response systems allow them to reveal their ignorance safely and get the feedback they need without revealing their misconceptions to everyone, as raising hands can do. Studies have in fact shown that anonymous response systems promote more feedback than raising hands or colored cards (Lantz, 2010).

Of course, it is vital that students understand that skills are gained through errors and feedback. Nearly two decades of work on the growth mindset by Carol Dweck and her colleagues have shown that students who believe intelligence can be molded by effort succeed far more than students who fall into the self-fulfilling prophecy of fixed intelligence and hold the belief that education (and much of life) is just the careful hiding of one's own ignorance (Dweck, 1999; Dweck, 2006).

A current line of research, much needed for CRSs, has focused on whether these systems can scaffold students into a growth mindset. Does consistent interaction with one's errors, and with one's peers, help teach students the invaluable lesson that the process of maturing as a learner is a process of revealing your errors and correcting them, that is, that intelligence is malleable? Likewise, through interacting with students' errors, can teachers and faculty come to a better understanding of how to encourage a growth mindset?

One group at the University of Massachusetts is creating a structure for teachers to learn peer-engaged, clicker-based pedagogy. The structure, called Technology Enhanced Formative Assessment (TEFA), focuses teachers on "question-driven instruction, dialogical discourse, formative assessment, and meta-level communication" (Beatty & Gerace, 2009, 146). This structure uses classroom response to focus on how students gain language fluency through communicating with each other.

Clicker Cases as an Alternative

Not all social interaction that uses clickers needs to be based on peer debate or tutoring. Lundeberg and colleagues (2011) have written about their use of clicker case studies across a number of universities' large biology courses.

They found that combining stories containing scientific messages with CRSs increased students' learning more than PowerPoint lectures. They also found that student performance especially improved where the cases created dissonance (related to giving feedback, as discussed earlier), captured attention, and involved students in interpreting data or making decisions (executive attention). The case studies focused on creating a cohesive lecture, based on a story of discovery and problem solving rather than a set of facts.

CONCLUSION: THE ENGAGED CLASSROOM OF THE FUTURE

Case-based teaching and peer tutoring create storylines of human interaction with other humans and the world, and they promote students' interaction with these storylines. This provides the opportunity for students to interact socially with the material, as they likely would in real life, giving their predictions social meaning. Other models, like TEFA, the Vanderbilt STAR Legacy Cycle, and Think-Pair-Share, incorporate three key items: individual struggle and conscious thought; discussion with a peer or peers, with feedback; and social sharing and feedback.

This basic framework can carry over to other situations as educational contexts change and classroom response begins to interact with other technologies. Other currently emerging technologies are attracting positive attention in current studies. Lecture capture (especially as mini-lectures and flipped classes), adaptive quizzing, wiki-based projects, vlogs, blogs, and social media all have benefits when used correctly. The most effective teachers with technology I have interacted with tend to select the best technological fit for their subject and context. Technologists and designers are now directing a fair portion of their effort toward making those contexts interact synergistically with each other.

The history of educational technology and educational psychology have overlapped at other times, as when B. F. Skinner created his "Skinnerian box," essentially a box of flash cards that quizzed students on the correct answer and proceeded to the next card only when this answer was given. Many of the details of this plan have changed, but the basic idea remains a part of our education today. Online flash card systems, adaptive quizzing systems, intermittent reinforcement systems, and even Mazur's ConcepTests work on the same basic idea of responsive quizzing that responds and adapts to individuals, guiding them along a formative path. The addition of case-based and peer tutoring models contributes a social dimension to this behaviorist feedback system.

As long as the skills needed by our education are social, the context of our education is likely to remain social—and a social education requires social technologies. CRSs are a social and psychological educational technology that fits easily and simply into many current educational contexts. Given proper design from vendors, CRSs can adapt to new possibilities. The large, open-course platform Coursera, for example, is beginning to integrate quizzing and polling into its video. Adobe is doing the same in videoconferencing. Classroom response questions could be integrated into these with future tools, as they can into discussion boards (and advanced discussion platforms, like Piazza). These integrations will require closer collaborations among groups creating CRSs, other developers of educational software, and the teachers and designers using these systems. For now, developing strong CRSs with an understanding of how students learn from them can prepare teachers for meaningful pedagogy today, tomorrow, and in the future.

NOTE

1. For readers interested in more detail, ConcepTests and the accompanying peer instruction model were recently reviewed by Vickrey et al. (2015) with specific recommendations about high and low technology options, and what parts of peer instruction are most necessary.

REFERENCES

Bangert-Drowns, R. L., Kulik, C. L. C., Kulik, J. A., & Morgan, M. (1991). The instructional effect of feedback in test-like events. *Review of educational research, 61*(2), 213–238.

Beatty, I. D., & Gerace, W. J. (2009). Technology-enhanced formative assessment: A research-based pedagogy for teaching science with classroom response technology. *Journal of Science Education and Technology, 18*(2), 146–162.

Beyer, C., Taylor, E., & Gillmore, G. M. (2013). *Inside the undergraduate teaching experience: The University of Washington's growth in faculty teaching study.* Albany, NY: State University of New York Press.

Broderick, M. (2009). *On the road to ROI.* Turning Technologies white paper. Youngstown, OH. Retrieved June 28, 2014, from http://meetingsupport.org/files/Turning%20Technologies%20ARS%20ROI%20Whitepaper%20(1).pdf

Bruff, D. (2009). *Teaching with classroom response systems: Creating active learning environments.* San Francisco, CA: Jossey-Bass.

Collins, J. (2008). Audience response systems: Technology to engage learners. *Journal of the American College of Radiology, 5*(9), 993–1000.

Crouch, C. H., & Mazur, E. (2001). Peer instruction: Ten years of experience and results. *American Journal of Physics, 69*(9), 970–977.

Dewey, J. (1997). Democracy and education: An introduction to the philosophy of education. New York, NY: The Free Press. (Original work published 1916)

Diamond, M., & Hopson, J. L. (1999). *Magic trees of the mind.* New York, NY: Plume.

Ding, L., Reay, N. W., Lee, A., & Bao, L. (2008). Effects of testing conditions on conceptual survey results. *Physics Education Research, 4*(1), 010112. Retrieved June 26, 2014 from http://physics.ohio-state.edu/~lbao/Papers/PRST-PER_2008-6-e010112-TestCondition.pdf

Dweck, C. S. (1999). *Self-theories: Their role in motivation, personality and development.* Philadelphia, PA: Taylor & Francis/Psychology Press.

Dweck, C. S. (2006). *Mindset: The new psychology of success.* New York, NY: Random House.

Edlund, J., Gustafson, J., Heldner, M., & Hjalmarsson, A. (2008). Towards human-like spoken dialogue systems. *Speech Communication, 50*(8), 630–645.

Elias, P. L., & Esswein, J. (2012). *U.S. Patent Application 13/586,762.*

Engert, F., & Bonhoeffer, T. (1999). Dendritic spine changes associated with hippocampal long-term synaptic plasticity. *Nature, 399*(6731), 66–70.

Ericsson, K. A. (2006). The influence of experience and deliberate practice on the development of superior expert performance. In K. A. Ericsson, Charness, N., Hoffman, R. R., & Feltovich, P. J., *The Cambridge handbook of expertise and expert performance (pp. 683–703).* Cambridge: Cambridge University Press.

Fischer, M., Kaech, S., Knutti, D., & Matus, A. (1998). Rapid actin-based plasticity in dendritic spines. *Neuron, 20*(5), 847–854.

Frase, L. T., Patrick, E., & Schumer, H. (1970). Effect of question position and frequency upon learning from text under different levels of incentive. *Journal of Educational Psychology, 61,* 52–56.

Freeman, S., Eddy, S. L., McDonough, M., Smith, M. K., Okoroafor, N., Jordt, H., & Wenderoth, M. P. (2014). Active learning increases student performance in science, engineering, and mathematics. *Proceedings of the National Academy of Sciences, 111*(23), 8410–8415.

Giacomini, C., Lyle, H., Wynn, W., Stahl, H., & Hankins, L. (2011). *Surveys on learning and scholarly technologies: Final report.* Retrieved June 27, 2014, from https://www.washington.edu/itconnect/wp-content/uploads/2013/12/Teaching-Learning-Research-Tech-2011-Full-Report.pdf

Giacomini, C., Wallis, P., Lyle, H., Haaland, W., Davis, K., & Comden, D. (2013, August). *Exploring eTextbooks at the University of Washington: What we learned and what is next.* Retrieved June 27, 2014, from https://www.washington.edu/itconnect/wp-content/uploads/2013/10/UWeTextCampusReport.pdf

Guthrie R., & Carlin, A. (2004). Waking the dead: Using interactive technology to engage passive listeners in the classroom. *Proceedings of the Tenth Americas Conference on Information Systems,* New York, NY, 1–8. Retrieved December 15, 2014, from http://www.mhhe.com/cps/docs/CPSWP_WakindDead082003.pdf

Jensen, E. (2008). *Brain-based learning: The new paradigm of teaching.* Thousand Oaks, CA: Corwin Press.

Kay, R. H., & LeSage, A. (2009). Examining the benefits and challenges of using audience response systems: A review of the literature. *Computers & Education, 53*(3), 819–827.

Kornell, N., Hays, M. J., & Bjork, R. A. (2009). Unsuccessful retrieval attempts enhance subsequent learning. *Journal of Experimental Psychology: Learning, Memory, and Cognition, 35*(4), 989–998.

Kruschke, J. K. (2003). Attention in learning. *Current Directions in Psychological Science, 12*(5), 171–175.

Kulhavy, R. W. (1977). Feedback in written instruction. *Review of Educational Research, 47*(1), 211–232.

Lantz, M. E. (2010). The use of "clickers" in the classroom: Teaching innovation or merely an amusing novelty? *Computers in Human Behavior, 26*(4), 556–561.

Lasry, N. (2008). Clickers or flashcards: Is there really a difference? *Physics Teacher, 46*(4), 242–244.

Lundeberg, M. A., Kang, H., Wolter, B., delMas, R., Armstrong, N., Borsari, B., . . . Herreid, C. F. (2011). Context matters: Increasing understanding with interactive clicker case studies. *Educational Technology Research and Development, 59*(5), 645–671.

Markman, A. (2012). *Smart thinking: Three essential keys to solve problems, innovate, and get things done.* New York, NY: Penguin.

Medina, J. (2008). *Brain rules: 12 principles for surviving and thriving at work, home, and school.* Seattle, WA: Pear Press.

Moser, J. S., Moran, T. P., Schroder, H. S., Donnellan, M. B., & Yeung, N. (2013). On the relationship between anxiety and error monitoring: A meta-analysis and conceptual framework. *Frontiers in Human Neuroscience, 7.* Retrieved May 26, 2015, from http://journal.frontiersin.org/article/10.3389/fnhum.2013.00466/full

Moser, J. S., Schroder, H. S., Heeter, C., Moran, T. P., & Lee, Y.-H. (2011). Mind your errors: Evidence for a neural mechanism linking growth mindset to adaptive posterior adjustments. *Psychological Science, 22,* 1484–1489.

Muller, D. A. (2008). *Designing effective multimedia for physics education* (Doctoral dissertation). University of Australia, Sydney.

National Research Council. (2000). *How people learn: Brain, mind, experience, and school* (Expanded ed.). Washington, DC: The National Academies Press.

Petersen, S. E., & Posner, M. I. (2012). The attention system of the human brain: 20 years after. *Annual Review of Neuroscience, 35,* 73–89.

Posner, M. I. (1980). Orienting of attention. *Quarterly Journal of Experimental Psychology, 32*(1), 3–25.

Posner, M. I. (2012). *Attention in a social world.* Oxford: Oxford University Press.

Reay, N. W., Bao, L., Warnakulasooriya, R., & Baugh, G. (2006). Toward the effective use of voting machines in physics lectures. *American Journal of Physics, 73*(6), 554–558.

Reay, N. W., Li, P., & Bao, L. (2008). Testing a new voting machine question methodology. *American Journal of Physics, 76*(2), 171–178.

Saettler, L. P. (1967). *A history of instructional technology.* New York, NY: McGraw-Hill.

Simmons, W. W., & Elsberry, R. B. (1988). *Inside IBM: The Watson years: A personal memoir.* Pittsburgh: Dorrance.

Sousa, D. A. (2012). *How the brain learns.* Thousand Oaks, CA: Corwin Press.

Thalheimer, W. (2003, January). *The learning benefits of questions.* Somerville, MA: Work Learning Research. Retrieved from http://www.newleafpartners.com/pdf/articles/learningbenefitsofquestions.pdf

Vane, E. T., & Gross, L. S. (1994). *Programming for TV, radio, and cable.* Boston, MA: Focal Press.

Vickrey, T., Rosploch, K., Rahmanian, R., Pilarz, M., & Stains, M. (2015). Research-based implementation of peer instruction: A literature review. *CBE—Life Sciences Education, 14*(1), es3. doi:10.1187/cbe.14-11-0198

Wallace, S. (Ed.). (2009). Vygotsky, Lev. In *A Dictionary of Education.* (p. 322). Oxford: Oxford University Press.

2

Who's in the Room?

Using Clickers to Assess Students' Needs, Attitudes, and Prior Knowledge

Traci Freeman and Brian Vanden Heuvel

We have all had the experience of preparing a lecture for a class, complete with clicker questions that encourage students' participation and active engagement. Ten or fifteen minutes into the lecture, we ask our first question. We anxiously await students' clicker responses. Staring up at the screen, we are met with the results of our labor—a histogram that is completely flat. In the moment, we stop to consider if our question is unclear. We scan it quickly for errors and to check our wording. Other classes have managed to respond to this question appropriately, so we feel confident that the question isn't the problem. We recognize that students might simply be disengaged and have clicked a random button rather than thinking through the problem, but we fear that we have not successfully delivered our instruction, and that our students may have failed to grasp the material.

When we use clickers in our classrooms, we have an opportunity to gain insight into the experiences of our students. Yet, the insights we gain are dependent on our ability to access the right information and reach the appropriate conclusions with the information we receive. Moreover, once we have this information, we need to know how to adapt our instruction to meet the needs we identify. Clicker technologies alone do not ensure effective teaching and learning. When clickers are used successfully, they simply facilitate teaching practices that are sound in their own right (Draper & Brown, 2004; Gray & Steer, 2012).

Although clickers possessed some initial novelty—a factor that correlates with increased student engagement (Draper & Brown, 2004; Lantz 2010)—during the last 10 years, they have become a common feature at most universities. Although the excitement around this technology may have waned, research continues to support the positive effects of clicker use, especially in teaching contexts that have traditionally been defined by didactic methods of instruction (Kay & LeSage, 2009). Clickers support better learning outcomes because they enable shifts in pedagogy that are consistent with theories of learning and best practices in instruction (Draper & Brown, 2004; Gray & Steer, 2012).

A significant body of scholarship has suggested that learning is dependent on individual students' needs, dispositions, and prior knowledge (Ambrose, Bridges, Dipietro, Lovett, & Norman, 2010; Marzano, 2007). To teach students successfully, instructors need to understand what students know— or need to know—about a subject, as well as how students feel about their learning. Instructional interventions geared toward accessing this information about students fall under the broader category of *formative assessment*. Clickers can operate effectively as tools for gaining formative data about students, especially in teaching contexts that make it difficult for instructors to know their students on an individual basis. Although clickers enable data collection, they do not tell instructors what information to collect, how to interpret this information, and how to proceed in a classroom once they collect this data. Using clickers in formative assessment requires a deeper understanding of factors that affect students' learning and of options available for individualizing instruction.

In this chapter, we argue that many of the benefits in student learning that we attribute to clickers may result from their role in formative assessment. We describe strategies for using clickers to gain information about students' needs, attitudes, and prior knowledge. Clicker technologies have facilitated access in real time to information about students' learning, but gaining information about learning is only part of the teaching and learning challenge. Once instructors and students have this information, we have to know what to do with it. This chapter focuses on two practices—contingent or "just-in-time" teaching and peer teaching—as theoretically informed pedagogies that capitalize on clicker technology.

FORMATIVE ASSESSMENT AND STUDENT LEARNING

One of the most powerful features of clickers is that they enable us to access real-time formative feedback about student learning. Any assessment can be used formatively if it is used to gather information about students' understanding and performance and prompts adjustments in teaching and learning. The term *formative assessment*, however, most frequently refers to assessments that are administered while students are in the process of learning new material (Marzano, 2007). Such feedback can be critical for instructors who are designing and delivering lessons and for students who are refining their knowledge and skills (Ambrose et al., 2010). Instructors can use formative data to make decisions about what new information or concepts they need to review or cover in depth and what concepts they need not invest time in discussing (Sun, Martinez, & Seli, 2014). Students can use formative feedback to assess their own knowledge, practice problem solving, and gain mastery of a subject. Students who can internalize and respond to the feedback they receive can develop as self-regulated learners (Black & William, 1998; Nicol & Macfarlane-Dick, 2006), a valuable metacognitive skill.

An important aspect of formative assessment is that it capitalizes on constructivist assumptions about learning (Black & William, 1998). As we have shifted away from thinking about teaching as the transmission and reception of knowledge and have adopted a more active view of learners, the role of formative assessment practices has become more central in teaching. Rather than viewing learning as a process in which students receive new information, we now understand that students learn by assimilating new knowledge in their already existing knowledge structures or schema or by accommodating new knowledge by transforming their current understanding (Ambrose et al., 2010; Piaget, 1964; Vygotsky, 1978). Students learn when they have strong foundations of prior knowledge, and this prior knowledge is activated in a learning context. When new information is presented in a way that allows students to easily assimilate it or when the introduction of new information forces students to revise their existing schema, they learn effectively. When students' prior knowledge is insufficient for the task they are engaging in, inappropriate for the context, or simply inaccurate, students have difficulty learning new information (Ambrose et al., 2010). Formative assessments can be instrumental in student learning because they can provide both instructors and students with information about students' prior knowledge, current understanding, and possible misconceptions, all of which can promote or interfere with students' acquisition of new knowledge. Tests, quizzes, and other assessments offer instructors and students feedback on what students are learning, but too often, the feedback from these assessments arrives too late for instructors to address students' needs and for students to identify their knowledge gaps and address their misconceptions (Black & William, 1998). Formative assessments that provide real-time feedback or feedback that is proximal to learning enable more responsive teaching practices. They also give students feedback on their learning and performance that can assist students in regulating their own learning and promote metacognitive awareness and help-seeking (Magaña & Marzano, 2014).

Although students' prior knowledge is critical in future learning, students' dispositions are also instrumental. Students' values and beliefs, motivations, and self-concepts also affect their learning (Ambrose et al., 2010; Dweck 2006; Han & Finkelstein, 2013). Formative assessments can be used to gain an understanding about the dispositions of students, and instructors can capitalize on this information to develop more relevant and engaging learning activities.

Reviews of the research focused on formative assessment underscore its power as an instructional strategy (Black & William, 1998; Marzano, 2007). As Marzano (2007) argued, instructional interventions involving formative assessment have more significant effects than any other instructional intervention. Formative assessments have the potential to transform the instructional dynamic, promoting knowledge transfer and students' agency as learners (Jones, Antonenkot, & Greenwood, 2012) and enabling contingent or just-in-time teaching (Simkins & Maier, 2009; Sun, Martinez, & Seli, 2014).

Arguably, one of the chief benefits of clickers is that they enable formative assessment in real time, especially in large classes where timely information about students' learning is difficult to access. When faculty use clickers in formative assessment, students report that the technology affects their learning and engagement more than when faculty use clickers in summative assessments, such as tests and quizzes (Han & Finkelstein, 2013). Yet, the technology alone is not responsible for the benefits witnessed when instructors incorporate clickers in their classrooms. To be effective, clickers must lead in some way to modifications in instruction (Black & William, 1998) and to changes students' behaviors. To capitalize on this technology, instructors need to understand how to ask good questions and access the information they need when this information will be most useful. They also need to understand what options are available to them once they have received feedback from students.

WHAT YOU NEED TO KNOW ABOUT YOUR STUDENTS TO TEACH THEM

Contemporary theories of education view the process of learning as a complicated phenomenon involving cognitive, social, psychological, and behavioral factors (Ambrose et al., 2010). Such conceptions mark a departure from behaviorist theories that characterize learning as a conditioned response to a stimulus. Although we have made dramatic shifts in the way we understand learning, our teaching practices, even with novel technologies such as clickers, seem grounded in earlier ideas about learning. If the clicker questions that accompany textbooks reflect common teaching practices, clickers are used most frequently in classes to drill students on their command of facts and not to gain formative data.

This is not to say that asking fact-based questions is ineffective as a teaching strategy, or that fact-based questions cannot provide meaningful formative feedback. If knowledge of facts represents a desired learning outcome, then fact-based questions are appropriate. For example, in anatomy and physiology, an instructor might want students to accurately name the bones in the skeletal system. In this case, fact-based questions match the instructor's learning goals and provide students with an understanding of how they are progressing toward achieving these goals. As an instructional intervention, frequent quizzing may facilitate students' learning of facts (Ambrose et al., 2010; Black & William, 1998). Deployed strategically, fact-based questions can also serve to prime students for the application and transfer of factual knowledge from one context to another (Jones et al., 2012).

Students' simple recall of facts, however, may not provide instructors with sufficient evidence that students understand underlying concepts. Without conceptual understanding, students may have a difficult time transferring their knowledge to new situations. For example, one of us, Brian Vanden Heuvel, taught students enrolled in an introductory biology class the concept of *natural selection*. Students were able to identify the correct definition in a multiple choice question, but when these same students were asked to predict what a population might look like in 10 generations as a result of natural selection, they were unable to answer the question. In this way, fact-based questions, used as formative assessment, can mislead instructors about students' command of course material.

Employing clickers for the purposes of formative assessment, then, will most likely require instructors to move beyond using clickers as a mechanism for quizzing students about facts. Useful formative data provides more nuanced information about students' experiences as learners, prior knowledge, misconceptions, motivations, and affective dispositions. Accessing this kind of formative data can help instructors see past the content they are teaching and respond to the needs of the students in the room.

Clicker questions that ask students to extend, apply, or synthesize their learning may provide more information about students' understanding than fact-based questions and may more accurately represent the deeper learning we value (Dangel & Wang, 2008). When students are asked to explore the implications of their learning and apply their knowledge, they are also more likely to be developing metacognitive awareness (Nicol & Macfarlane-Dick, 2006). Questions that ask students to reason through scenarios, solve authentic problems, and probe the implications of their knowledge help them reflect more deeply on their thinking. They also help instructors check whether students have internalized and can apply concepts. For example, an instructor could describe a farmer's field, including specific conditions related to moisture, day length, and temperature. To prompt students' synthesis and application of knowledge, an instructor might give students a choice of four different crops and ask, "What crop will grow best in this farmer's field?" To answer this question, students will need to draw from their understanding of photosynthesis, plant diversity, and anatomy, and apply this knowledge to solve an authentic problem. Questions like this, which require students to operationalize their knowledge and describe and defend their thinking, provide instructors with formative data and reveal misconceptions that may be interfering with students' understanding.

Questions that are designed explicitly to uncover common misconceptions are particularly useful in formative assessment. Although scholarship about misconceptions once held that misconceptions always interfere with the acquisition of new knowledge, we now understand that misconceptions can also be useful or productive in new learning (Maskiewicz & Lineback, 2013). Students' initial, naïve ideas might offer structures that can be refined and built upon, but in order to address students' misconceptions productively, an instructor must first identify them and understand how they may be operating for students. For example, students often mistakenly believe that the process of natural selection produces what an organism desires: a cheetah is fast because it "wants to be fast," not because speed confers an advantage that is selected for. To help students identify and address the problem with their thinking, instructors need to ask questions that uncover this misconception, and they should use the opportunity to help students understand that the population responds to pressures and advantages and that organisms cannot independently shape their futures.

Asking students multiple questions that require them to apply their knowledge to different situations also helps students establish the limits of a particular concept and develop mastery of the material. For example, when Vanden Heuvel teaches the concept of photosynthesis, he asks students a number of fact-based questions: "What pigments absorb?" "Do pigments absorb all wavelengths of light equally?" "What wavelengths do plants absorb?" Then he asks students the question, "Why are plants green?" As students are able to apply their knowledge to solve increasingly difficult problems, instructors gain more confidence in their students' learning and can more readily identify the limits of their students' understanding.

Most of the recommended interventions using clickers focus on the cognitive dimensions of learning. Clickers can be used to assess students' understanding of facts, their ability to apply their knowledge to solve authentic problems, their misconceptions and the limits of their understanding. Clickers, however, might also be employed effectively to collect formative data on noncognitive factors that affect learning—dispositional factors like students' motivations, engagement, beliefs, values, and attitudes. This is perhaps one of the least studied uses of clickers in the classroom, but it has considerable potential to transform instruction. As we have come to understand the profound effects that noncognitive factors have on students' learning and performance (Dweck, 2006; Graesser & D'Mello, 2012), we might consider how collecting formative data on dispositional factors might be used in our instruction.

For example, clickers might be used to foster student engagement by leveraging the interests of students in the room. Questions that address students' motivations for taking the class or for learning specific concepts can provide instructors with valuable information that they can use when they craft lectures or search for examples. Clickers can also provide instructors with feedback about students' affective dispositions toward learning. Although a certain amount of confusion or perplexity can motivate learning, when students' confusion turns to frustration, they may be more inclined to disengage from lectures and less likely to process new material effectively (Graesser & D'Mello, 2012). Clicker questions that uncover students' levels of frustration provide instructors with information about pacing or with clues about when students might need additional time or examples to process new information. Although it is not common practice, asking students about their interest in the material or their own emotional relationship to their learning provides instructors with potentially useful information, which is difficult to access in any classroom, but especially in large groups.

STRATEGIES OF CONTINGENT OR JUST-IN-TIME TEACHING AND PEER INSTRUCTION

One of the chief benefits of clicker technologies is that they enable us to gather information about our students' learning in real time. The instructional challenge, however, lies in interpreting and responding to the information we receive, particularly if we are used to employing didactic teaching methods in large lecture halls. When we develop lectures, we make assumptions about what students know and will need to know to understand new concepts or processes, and we structure our lectures based on our assumptions. Yet, if we are mistaken, we may fail in our instructional aims and learn only too late that we have failed when students struggle with tests, quizzes, and homework problems. Soliciting questions at key moments in a lecture or stopping periodically during instruction to ask students questions and check their understanding can provide some provisional information about students' comprehension, but these strategies do not afford instructors a sense of the whole class's experience. Clickers are able to give us more complete information, but they do not alone constitute an adequate instructional intervention.

When instructors do learn that students may not be understanding material or when they uncover students' misconceptions, they have some strategies available to them. Consider this example. In the fall of 2010, Vanden Heuvel was teaching a large introductory biology course for majors at a midsized regional university. Students included more than 200 first-year biology majors who had satisfied the prerequisite of at least one year of high school biology. After finishing a 15-minute introduction to Mendelian genetics, Vanden Heuvel proceeded to ask a series of five multiple-choice clicker questions. After each question, he posted a histogram of the classroom responses, allowing the students to see how the entire class answered each question. This particular set of students showed an equal distribution for each answer, indicating either that students were disengaged and simply guessing or that they believed each of the answers represented a viable response to each of the questions.

When confronted with these results, Vanden Heuvel asked the students to try to convince a partner that their answers were correct. He emphasized that even if students were guessing when they chose their answers, they were still likely making choices because of something in the question, perhaps a word or phrase that offered an association with a concept. After one minute, students re-voted on the same set of clicker questions. Typically, when Vanden Heuvel asks students to re-vote after they have discussed their responses with other students, he sees a dramatic improvement in the classroom data. He finds either that most students select a single "correct" answer or that students are evenly split in their responses between two answers. If the students are split in their responses, he asks them to explain to the larger group why they would select one option over another, which gives him an opportunity to check for specific conceptual or procedural errors, and then he identifies the correct response.

Vanden Heuvel often finds peer instruction to be an effective strategy to address gaps in students' learning, evidenced by students' ability to demonstrate their understanding in subsequent questions. In fact, involving students in peer instruction following clicker responses is a recommended best practice (Stewart & Stewart, 2013). In this particular instance, however, when students re-voted, he saw once again an equal distribution of responses. With this new information, having witnessed the failure of peer instruction to address students' problems with the material, Vanden Heuvel knew he had to do something else, but his options were limited. He could review the slides from the first 15 minutes of the lecture, but he realized immediately that doing so would probably be an exercise in futility. If the lecture content failed to produce results the first time he delivered it, it was unlikely to do so a second time. He could step away from the PowerPoint and attempt to "chalk talk" students through the concepts, but he had not prepared additional strategies for explaining the concepts, and he did not have enough information from students' responses to his clicker questions to identify exactly where students were getting stuck.

Vanden Heuvel made a split-second decision to close the lecture and pull up students' homework problems. For the remainder of class, students worked in groups on their homework while he circulated among them. Students were able to practice applying their knowledge and could receive immediate feedback from their partners and from him about their answers. Working through problems helped students to develop a deeper understanding of the concepts and to identify significant conceptual and procedural errors. At the beginning of the next lecture, Vanden Heuvel asked students to respond to another set of clicker questions related to the previous lesson, and students' responses indicated that they understood the topic.

Vanden Heuvel's experience illustrates the benefits and challenges of using clickers in formative assessment. As other research has suggested, clickers provide instructors with real-time feedback that enables them to address students' needs through contingent or just-in-time teaching (Sun, Martinez, & Seli, 2014). Contingent teaching uses student feedback to structure lessons and respond to students' authentic needs for instruction rather than using a predetermined lesson (Draper & Brown, 2004). The idea of contingent teaching is supported by social constructivist theories, which hold that learning takes place in a student's zone of proximal development, that is, in the space between what students know and can do on their own and what they need guidance to learn or accomplish (Vygotsky, 1978). Understanding the foundational knowledge that students possess helps instructors operate effectively within students' zones of proximal development and identify misconceptions before students internalize them. Contingent teaching enhances instruction because it helps instructors make good use of class time by prioritizing topics in discussions, illuminating students' misconceptions, and, when paired with peer instruction, fostering students' classroom interactions (Kay & LeSage, 2009).

Research also supports the efficacy of peer instruction in teaching and learning (Topping, 1996). Peer instruction leverages the power of students in the group to provide reciprocal feedback on each other's learning (Boud,

Cohen, & Sampson, 2001). It represents a departure from the typical lecture format characteristic of most postsecondary instruction and results in a more active, collaborative, and problem-based method of instruction. Peer feedback works best when students are asked to apply a concept or solve problems alone or in small groups and then explain their reasoning to others (Crouch & Mazur, 2001). As an intervention, peer learning has both cognitive and emotional effects, increasing students' critical thinking and capacity for applying their knowledge, as well as their motivation (Baud, Cohen, & Sampson, 2001). Clicker questions provide an opportunity for faculty to incorporate peer instruction into their lectures and can be effective in offering just-in-time instruction in large classroom settings, where it is impossible for an instructor to address every student during the course of a class.

As Vanden Heuvel's experience also demonstrates, however, contingent teaching and peer instruction present instructors with some challenges. These teaching strategies demand a certain kind of flexibility from instructors. Rather than imagining a lecture as a linear progression through a series of related concepts, instructors might need to structure their lectures as "branching" plans, where students' responses to material determine the course of the lecture (Draper & Brown, 2004). Structuring a class this way is complicated and potentially messy. Rather than designing only one lesson for each class, an instructor may need to prepare several lessons designed to address the common issues students might experience when they learn a topic—and to be ready to shuttle among these lessons based on students' responses.

An additional issue might be the use of PowerPoint and other presentation software as a standard for lectures. Such programs make shuttling back and forth even more difficult, because they are linear in their organization. Although these programs have enabled more sophisticated visual and multimedia components to be incorporated into lectures, they have also made the lecture structure more rigid and made it more difficult for instructors to go off script, backtrack, or supplement instruction based on students' needs. As Vanden Heuvel discovered, if students fail to grasp material after working through every planned contingency, instructors may be at a loss. Although he was able to recover and, with some quick thinking, engage students in an activity that was instrumental in their learning, he also lost most of a lecture and had to reduce the amount of material that he would cover in the class.

Similarly, peer instruction, although a recommended best practice, is not always effective. As many critics of peer-centered pedagogies have noted, it can at times seem like "the blind leading the blind." If students leave a peer-mediated discussion with their misconceptions reinforced, they may have a difficult time revising their understanding.

To use clickers effectively in formative assessment, we need to do more than simply stop periodically throughout a lecture to ask students a few questions. We need to have an instructional goal in mind that clickers help us to realize. We need to know what kinds of student information we should acquire and what this information might communicate about our students' learning, and we need techniques to help us respond in real time to what our students tell us. To implement strategies in support of contingent teaching and peer learning, instructors need to reconceptualize the way they build their lectures; learn to identify common sticking points for students; come to classes with flexible plans and extra activities and problems; and be willing to forgo coverage for deeper kinds of learning. We need to shift from thinking about teaching as the act of communicating content to recognizing that teaching requires that we understand who is in the room.

REFERENCES

Ambrose, S. A., Bridges, M. W., Dipietro, M., Lovett, M., & Norman, M. K. (2010). *How learning works: 7 research-based principles for smart teaching*. San Francisco, CA: Jossey-Bass.

Black, P., & William, D. (1998, March). Assessment and classroom learning. *Assessment in Education, Principles, Policy & Practice, 5*(1), 7–74. doi:10.1080/0969595980050102

Boud, D., Cohen, R., & Sampson, J. (Eds.). (2001). *Peer learning in higher education: Learning from and with each other*. New York, NY: Routledge.

Crouch, C. H., & Mazur, E. (2001). Peer instruction: Ten years of experience and results. *American Journal of Physics, 69*, 970–977. doi: 10.1119/1.374249

Dangel, H. L., & Wang, C. X. (2008). Student response systems in higher education: Moving beyond linear teaching and surface learning. *Journal of Educational Technology Development and Exchange, 1*(1), 93–104. Retrieved December 15, 2014, from http://www.sicet.org/journals/jetde/jetde08/paper08.pdf

Draper, S. W., & Brown, M. I. (2004). Increasing interactivity in an electronic voting system. *Computer Assisted Learning 20*(2), 81–94. doi: 10.1111/j.1365-2729.2004.00074.x

Dweck, C. S. (2006). *Mindset*. New York, NY: Random House.

Graesser, A. C., & D'Mello, S. (2012). 5 emotions during the learning of difficult material. *Psychology of Learning and Motivation-Advances in Research and Theory, 57*, 183–190.

Gray, K., & Steer, D. N. (2012). Personal response systems and learning: It is the pedagogy that matters, not the technology. *Journal of College Science Teaching, 41*(5), 80–88.

Han, J. H., & Finkelstein, A. (2013). Understanding the effects of professors' pedagogical development with clicker assessment and feedback technologies and the impact on students' engagement and learning in higher education. *Computers & Education, 65*, 64–76. doi: 10.1016/j.compedu.2013.02.002

Jones, M. E., Antonenkot, P. D., & Greenwood, C. M. (2012). The impact of collaborative and individualized student response system strategies on learner motivation, metacognition, and knowledge transfer. *Journal of Assisted Learning, 28*, 477–481. doi: 10.1111/j.1365-2729.2011.00470.x

Kay, R. H., & LeSage, A. (2009). Examining the benefits and challenges of using audience response systems: A review of the literature. *Computers & Education, 53*(3), 819–827.

Lantz, M. E. (2010). The use of "clickers" in the classroom: Teaching innovation or merely an amusing novelty? *Computers in Human Behavior, 26*(4), 556–561.

Magaña, S., & Marzano, R. J. (2014). *Enhancing the art & science of teaching with technology.* Bloomington, IN: Marzano Research Laboratory.

Marzano, R. J. (2007). *The art and science of teaching: A comprehensive framework for effective instruction.* Alexandria, VA: ASCD.

Maskiewicz, A. C., & Lineback, J. E. (2013). Misconceptions are "so yesterday." *CBE—Life Sciences Education, 12*(3), 352–356. doi:10.1187/cbe.13-01-0014

Nicol, D. J., & Macfarlane-Dick, D. (2006). Formative assessment and self-regulated learning: A model and seven principles of good feedback practice. *Studies in Higher Education, 31*(2), 199–208.

Piaget, J. (1964). Development and learning. In R. E. Ripple & V. N. Rockcastle (Eds.), *Piaget rediscovered* (pp. 7–20). Ithaca, NY: Cornell University Press.

Simkins, S., & Maier, M. H. (Eds.). (2009). *Just-in-time teaching: Across the disciplines, across the academy.* Sterling, VA: Stylus.

Stewart, S., & Stewart, B. (2013). Taking clickers to the next level: A contingent teaching model. *International Journal of Mathematical Education in Science and Technology, 44*(8), 1093–1106. doi: 10.1080/0020739X.2013.770086

Sun, J. C.-Y., Martinez, B., & Seli, H. (2014). Just-in-time or plenty-of-time teaching? Different electronic feedback devices and their effect on student engagement. *Educational Technology & Society, 17*(2), 234–244.

Topping, K. J. (1996). The effectiveness of peer tutoring in further and higher education: A typology and review of the literature. *Higher Education, 32*(3), 321–345.

Vygotsky, L. (1978). *Mind and Society.* Cambridge, MA: Harvard University Press.

3

Using Clickers in the Arts and Humanities

David S. Goldstein

Although classroom response systems (clickers) are gaining popularity in many disciplines—especially science, technology, engineering, and mathematics (STEM) fields, where most of the empirical research on clicker use has predictably taken place, including the influential work of Harvard physics professor Eric Mazur—few teachers of humanities and the arts consider using clickers. Not only can clickers be powerful learning aids in the humanities; they can also help reinvigorate student interest in humanities courses and better engage the students already enrolled in such courses, including those who, perhaps begrudgingly, take them to satisfy breadth requirements while pursuing other majors. I see no reason why clickers should be more heavily concentrated in STEM courses than in humanities courses. One might even argue that they are potentially more useful and important in the increasingly beleaguered humanities.

Despite a trend in the last two decades of declining enrollment in humanities majors and decreasing public support for the arts and humanities, I am in good (and learned) company when I assert that the humanities are as relevant and crucial as ever in a world that sometimes seems to have lost its mind. We can cite complex reasons for this apparent loss of interest in the humanities—the economy, the spiraling cost of higher education, the increasingly utilitarian view of the purpose of a college degree (Marcus, 2013), politically motivated antipathy (Delany, 2013), and so forth—but I feel that we faculty members are still in the business of educating world citizens who embody moral courage, understand diverse cultures, and pursue lifelong learning. The fact that the skills in critical thinking, problem solving, collaboration, and written and verbal communication happen to be quite marketable is a valuable benefit of a good, liberal education, but my aim, and that of most of my peers, is higher than that. I want our graduates to be deeply thoughtful, reflective human beings. The humanities—and, I would hasten to add, the arts—are not expendable luxuries.

The Commission on the Humanities (1980), funded by the Rockefeller Foundation, stated eloquently in its influential report, *The Humanities in American Life*, that

> the humanities mirror our own image and our image of the world. Through the humanities we reflect on the fundamental question: What does it mean to be human? The humanities offer clues but never a complete answer. They reveal how people have tried to make moral, spiritual, and intellectual sense of a world in which irrationality, despair, loneliness, and death are as conspicuous as birth, friendship, hope, and reason. We learn how individuals or societies define the moral life and try to attain it, attempt to reconcile freedom and the responsibilities of citizenship, and express themselves artistically. The humanities do not necessarily mean humaneness, nor do they always inspire the individual with what Cicero called "incentives to noble action." But by awakening a sense of what it might be like to be someone else or to live in another time or culture, they tell us about ourselves, stretch our imagination, and enrich our experience. They increase our distinctively human potential. (p. 1)

I can do little to alter the trend of the declining number of humanities majors and interest in elective humanities courses, but I can do my best to inspire the students I do have in my literature and film studies courses. Rather than jealously denigrate technology, however, I embrace it wherever it might improve student learning. Two decades of teaching experience have convinced me that classroom response systems—clickers—can powerfully enhance students' engagement with sophisticated and complex concepts in the humanities, perhaps especially for students who are *not* humanities majors. I would like to offer one course, an advanced film studies course on queer cinema, as a case in point, although I have had similarly salutary results in other courses, such as Exploring American Culture: Race, Ethnicity, and Immigration, and Ethnic American Literatures.

My queer cinema course strives to help students understand at least a bit more about the range and complexity of human experiences that occupy and animate the humanities. As I note on the syllabus, the course examines films "that not only challenge prevailing sexual norms, but [also] seek to undermine the very categories of gender and sex that our culture perpetuates." I further claim that, as a medium "that intentionally and unintentionally reflects and shapes our perceptions of sexual categories and norms, film has been a powerful aspect of American culture for a century and merits our careful study."

Toward those ends, I enumerate on the syllabus the course's learning goals:

1. develop a fundamental understanding of contemporary queer theory
2. develop the ability to discuss and analyze the complex interrelationship between attitudes toward sex and sexuality and cinematic representations of those attitudes
3. develop the ability to speak and write critically about theoretical and historical issues and concepts regarding sexual identity in cinema
4. develop the ability to interpret in sophisticated ways—informed by a neoformalist approach—the ideology and ideological subtext of selected American films
5. develop the ability to locate and assess sources, using a range of information literacy skills, to inform film analysis and interpretation

I can confidently state that clickers were essential in achieving nearly all of these learning goals.

Because human sexuality can be a touchy subject, I used clickers in the first class meeting to elicit from students some aspects of their own sexual orientation as well as some of their attitudes toward sexuality. I felt that if students knew the diversity of experience and opinions among their classmates, they could be more mindful of what they said, and perhaps more willing to consider viewpoints other than their own. I also thought that students should be aware if a particular viewpoint they held put them in a small minority so they could make an informed decision about what to disclose; although I encourage students to share minority views, I wanted them to do so with intention. Of course, asking for a show of hands would be quite awkward. I could not simply ask for students to raise their hands if they identified as, for example, bisexual, or if they thought straight people were typically prejudiced. So instead, I used clickers.

At my institution of about 5,000 students, we have two sets of 40 handheld clickers, which faculty members can reserve and borrow from our Office of Learning Technologies. Our School of Science, Technology, Engineering, and Mathematics requires its students to purchase clickers at the bookstore because they use clickers fairly often, but clickers are used less frequently in the other schools on campus, including mine, the School of Interdisciplinary Arts and Sciences, so I prefer to borrow clickers rather than require students to buy them. The Office of Learning Technologies' clicker sets are from Turning Technologies, a popular manufacturer of clicker sets and accompanying software. The software enables instructors to integrate poll questions into

PowerPoint slides. Because the software can be downloaded for free, I can create clicker questions for PowerPoint anywhere I have access to the PowerPoint application—in my campus office, in my home, on my laptop at a café, or even on my tablet or smartphone. Once instructors get fairly adept at creating the slides, they can even create them on the fly, in the classroom.

Using the Turning Technologies software, I created poll questions such as the following:

- I primarily identify as:
  1. gay, lesbian, or homosexual
  2. bisexual
  3. straight
  4. transgendered
  5. queer
  6. other

- I feel that:
  1. homosexuality goes against my religious beliefs.
  2. homosexuality is wrong for reasons other than religious.
  3. homosexuality is okay, but it makes me uncomfortable.
  4. homosexuality is okay, and it doesn't bother me.
  5. homosexuality is preferable to heterosexuality.
  6. I have no opinion about homosexuality.

Not wanting to single out any one sexual identity, I also asked the same kinds of questions about heterosexuality, and so on.

In my class of 40 undergraduates—mostly juniors and seniors—the breakdown of responses roughly approximated those found in society at large, which made our classroom something of a microcosm. I would like to think, though, that our microcosm was a bit more sensitive and respectful than the larger society because (a) they knew one another as individuals, and (b) they have been reminded on the syllabus that "I hope and expect that no students will be reluctant to express their opinions because they fear being ridiculed, judged, or ostracized. Furthermore, your grade will not be affected by the content of your opinions. We need not agree with one another, but we must respect one another." Such a statement certainly is no guarantee of a safe space for discourse, but it establishes an expectation for which I can hold students accountable. Luckily, in this class—one of the riskiest ones I have taught—the students remained respectful throughout the term. I believe knowing a little about their classmates from the very first day helped establish that atmosphere.

Because the majors offered at my campus tend to be nontraditional and interdisciplinary, I knew my students were unlikely to have much background in cultural theory at all, let alone queer theory. We offer no film studies major, and only a handful of my students had matriculated in the closest major—culture, literature, and the arts. In fact, about a quarter of the students were business majors, not even in our school. I also knew that nearly all of the students would have little or no experience in cinema studies, despite the course being called "Topics in Advanced Cinema Studies" and offered at the 400 (senior) level. Clickers enabled me to confirm, easily and instantaneously, that nearly all of the students were new to film studies, simply by asking a few questions about previous coursework or other experiences in film studies. I therefore knew I would need to provide a foundation of both the theory and analytical skills used in formalist film studies. Moreover, as this was a summer session course and therefore only 8 weeks rather than the usual 10-week quarter, the students would need to quickly get up to speed on theory and skills.

To help provide the theoretical foundation they would need to analyze the course's films, I assigned some notoriously challenging, sophisticated essays in queer theory, including several from the Palgrave Macmillan volume *Queer Theory* (Morland & Willox, 2004); New York University Press's volume *Queer Theory: An Introduction* (Jagose, 1997); and Riki Wilchins's (2004) book *Queer Theory, Gender Theory: An Instant Primer*. By asking clicker questions about key ideas presented in the texts, I was able to immediately ascertain how well the students understood what they had read (or whether they read at all!).

Knowing instantaneously, at the beginning of a class period, what students comprehended and what they misunderstood, I was able to help dispel their confusion without wasting precious class time on concepts that gave them no trouble. Even a paper-based reading quiz would not have provided me with such immediate feedback, because I would have been unable to examine them until after that class period. Also, if only one or two students answered a clicker question incorrectly, I simply asked them to visit me during office hours. They knew they were in a minority and were willing to let the class move on to other topics. (Our clicker system permits individually identified responses, but, in this class, I used only anonymous responses. Although I did not know *which* students were struggling, *they* knew and were able to seek my assistance outside of class time.) I also used the clickers for a quick, informal, ungraded quiz on the university's academic integrity policy, which had been assigned reading, to underscore my serious expectations of their behavior.

We also used clickers after screening each film to provide a quick profile of the students' thoughts about the film. I could ask questions about formal elements of the film (e.g., "To what degree did the film's music affect your emotional response?" with a Likert scale of response choices) as well as about students' subjective responses to the film (e.g., "Compared to last week's film, did this one tell us less about the range of human sexual identity, about the same, or more?"). For example, we used clickers to probe the formal differences between Jamie Babbit's 1999 satirical comedy, *But I'm a Cheerleader!* (Creel, Sperling, & Babbit, 1999), and the Wachowski Brothers' dark 1996 thriller, *Bound* (Boros, Lazar, & The Wachowski Brothers, 1996), and our subsequent responses to those differences. We noted the intentional irony, for instance, of casting drag performer RuPaul as a straight, "pray-away-the-gay" camp counselor in *But I'm a Cheerleader!*, which augmented the film's campy and effective send-up of homophobia.

By using clickers to (painlessly) ascertain my students' comprehension of queer theory concepts and clarifying aspects that confused them, which also helped them write more sophisticated interpretive essays, we more readily achieved course learning goal 1 (develop a fundamental understanding of contemporary queer theory). By using clickers to help students recognize the formal elements of films and to practice "reading" the films with and against the "grain," we more readily achieved course learning goals 2 (develop the ability to discuss and analyze the complex interrelationship between attitudes toward sex and sexuality and cinematic representations of those attitudes), 3 (develop the ability to speak and write critically about theoretical and historical issues and concepts regarding sexual identity in cinema), and 4 (develop the ability to interpret in sophisticated ways—informed by a neoformalist approach—the ideology and ideological subtext of selected American films).

Clickers are imperfect tools. They enabled me to ask many kinds of questions, but forced students to choose from a finite set of responses, which sometimes oversimplified the information we were able to ascertain. For example, the questions about sexual identity had to be in forced-choice format, whereas sexual identity itself is much more nuanced and more continuous on several dimensions. Similarly, for reading comprehension questions, students could be unintentionally led away from a correct answer by a seductive but incorrect answer. I normally prefer short-answer quizzes and exams because I know I am too good at writing wrong responses, which compromise the validity of such assessment instruments as measures of student comprehension. With clickers, however, I had to present questions in multiple-choice format. Because the responses were low stakes, however (students' grades were unaffected), the assessment did not need to be precise, so I was willing to take that risk in order to reap the great benefit of instantaneous data.

With any technology, teachers must contend with occasional glitches. Every once in a while, a student's clicker did not work, and I would have to pause class to issue a new one. (The swap was quick because I was using anonymized responses and did not need to associate the device with the particular student.) I also would not recommend using clickers for graded quizzes in larger classes, because students can more easily enter responses for students other than themselves with little chance of being detected by the instructor.

The potential benefits of clickers, however, far outweigh their limitations. Frequent, timely assessments of student learning enable us to revise our teaching on the fly to meet students where they are at any given moment, which cannot help but improve student learning. Clickers therefore can be an invaluable tool in shifting our classes from teacher centered ("I am telling you this and therefore you know it") to learner centered ("I have discovered what you already know and will provide what you need to learn more"). And, by the way, when learning is more evident to students, which clickers can help accomplish, they tend to submit stronger course evaluations, a nice side benefit that is not inconsequential in a higher education milieu in which the evaporation of tenure leaves most of us more vulnerable, with less job security, from year to year. Mostly, though, we care about our students and rejoice in their greater learning.

REFERENCES

Boros, S. (Producer), Lazar, A. (Producer), & The Wachowski Brothers (Director). (1996). *Bound* [Motion picture]. United States: Gramercy Pictures.

Commission on the Humanities. (1980). *The humanities in American life: Report of the Commission on the Humanities.* Berkeley, CA: University of California Press. Retrieved September 13, 2014, from http://ark.cdlib.org/ark:/13030/ft8j49p1jc/

Creel, L. (Producer), Sperling, A. (Producer), & Babbit, J. (Director). (1999). *But I'm a cheerleader!* [Motion picture]. United States: Lions Gate Entertainment Corporation.

Delany, E. (2013, December 1). Humanities studies under strain around the globe. *New York Times.* Retrieved September 13, 2014, from www.nytimes.com/2013/12/02/us/humanities-studies-under-strain-around-the-globe.html

Jagose, A. (1997). *Queer theory: An introduction.* New York, NY: NYU Press.

Marcus, J. (2013, March 7). *In era of high costs, humanities come under attack.* The Hechinger Report. Retrieved September 13, 2014, from http://hechingerreport.org/content/in-era-of-high-costs-humanities-come-under-attack_11120/

Morland, I., & Willox, A. (Eds.). (2004). *Queer theory.* New York, NY: Palgrave Macmillan.

Wilchins, R. (2004). *Queer theory, gender theory: An instant primer.* New York, NY: Alyson Books.

4

Using Clickers in the Social Sciences

Ron Krabill

I faced a dilemma. After several years of teaching an interdisciplinary course designed to introduce students to social and political theory with an emphasis on approaches to social action, I was observing a consistent trend: Conservative students were not speaking up in class. Through personal conversations, end-of-course self-assessments, and grading of student essays, it became evident that more conservative students felt extremely reluctant to actively engage in class discussions. This trend had a clear, detrimental impact in the classroom: Students were limiting their own conversations to mimicking the "talking heads" they had observed in U.S. political media. Left-leaning students would sloppily repeat the arguments they had heard before, most often without thinking through the deeper assumptions or implications of those arguments or how they connected (or did not connect) to the readings for the day, whether those readings were by Thomas Hobbes, Martin Luther King Jr., Adam Smith, or Judith Butler. Right-leaning students would remain silent in the (mistaken) belief that they were one of only a very few such students in the class, thus building a protective wall around their own positions in order to retain them without testing their assumptions or implications. And more radical students, as well as students less committed to any particular ideological tradition, were left struggling to relate their classmates' positions to the content of the course itself.

So I turned to clickers. To many, this may seem a surprising move. How might clickers help deepen students' engagement with controversial topics such as ideology, political theory, and social change? Clickers have been shown to be extremely effective in testing student comprehension and increasing student engagement, as well as managing course logistics like attendance and tests, particularly in large classes. But this class, Institutions and Social Change, was medium sized with 45 students, and class attendance and overall engagement were high. How could clickers help to solve this teaching dilemma?

My experience with clickers indicates that they provide a technology to identify and explore issues of particular relevance to the social sciences. Clickers are uniquely suited to trouble the assumptions students often carry into the classroom around issues of class, race, gender, religion, income inequality, and political ideologies. They allow students to experiment with the framing of social science questions and the way research into such questions is communicated through social and mass media. And they allow a level of anonymity in responses that, if used carefully, can raise controversial subjects in a way that encourages students to rethink their own positions and respect the positions of their classmates.

INCONVENIENT FACTS AND SOCIAL AND POLITICAL IDENTITIES

One of the foundational thinkers in the social sciences, Max Weber, spoke of the need for the social scientist to confront what he called "inconvenient facts": those facts that stand in opposition to one's political and ideological beliefs or expectations. For Weber, and social scientists ever since, one of the fundamental tasks of social science is to understand and explain the social facts that surprise us given our assumptions about the world and how it operates. The counterintuitive observation thus becomes essential to expanding our understandings of the social world. Further complicating this dynamic, inconvenient facts are frequently tied closely to issues of identity and the often complicated relationships among social identities, personal perspectives, and political positions. How one identifies personally or socially often shapes subsequent assumptions and the particular constellation of facts that become inconvenient to that subject position.

Clickers, though, provide the opportunity to bring many of these assumptions to the surface within the microcosm of a social science course. Take, for instance, the classic example of class identity in the United States. As social scientists have long observed, the overwhelming majority of U.S. residents consider themselves "middle class." In my course, I asked students via clickers how they identify their own socioeconomic class—a question that would be very difficult to ask without the anonymity of clickers. Given the three options of upper class, middle class, and lower class, nearly all my students (96%) replied that they were middle class, with the remainder (4%) identifying as upper class. These results illustrated the trend toward identification as middle class far more effectively than anything I could have said as the instructor. I then disaggregated the middle and lower class categories into five categories—upper-middle class, middle class, lower-middle class, working class, and poor/underclass—while keeping upper class as a category. When students were polled using these new categories, the upper class respondents disappeared and the poor/underclass had no respondents. But 9% of the class identified as working class, with a relatively even distribution across the three middle class categories (26%, 30%, and 35%, respectively). When the students were polled again using a different nomenclature—rich, middle class, working class, and poor—10% of them identified as rich, 62% as middle class, 24% as working class, and 5% as poor. The shifting self-identifications of the students based solely on the wording of the questions and the previous responses of their classmates precipitated students' recognition of the shifting, permeable nature of these categories, how they are named, and what they purport to describe in the social world. Seeing this phenomenon firsthand, enabled by the use of clickers, the students learned experientially a critical idea in social science.

Following the questions around social class, I then asked a series of questions that focused more explicitly on income; again, these were questions I would have a difficult time asking without the anonymity of clickers. Here, I first asked about students' individual annual income, in increments of $20,000, including a last category of more than $100,000. Not surprisingly for a group of (mostly full-time) students, 70% of the class reported an annual income of less than $20,000 a year. But when I asked about annual income for the living unit of the student, we found a fairly even distribution in the categories above $20,000. I followed this question with one regarding the income of the household in which students were raised as children. When nearly one-third of the class responded with a household income of over $100,000, with the remainder distributed mostly between $20,000 and $60,000, there were audible gasps around the room. In that moment, students clearly understood that the assumptions they had made—that their fellow classmates had come from relatively similar class backgrounds—were not necessarily accurate. This permitted students in the ensuing discussion to dig much deeper into the experiences of people situated differently than themselves in terms of social class, rather than assuming a false commonality.

These questions around social class are just one example among many of how clickers helped provide a moment for students to self-identify anonymously as part of a social category that they may previously have believed applied only to themselves. The clickers repeatedly allowed students to surprise themselves (and each other) by recognizing that a class of just 45 students included a much more diverse set of life experiences than might have been obvious from outward appearances. As with social class, students discovered they were not alone in a wide variety of identities and experiences, including sexuality, gender identities, receipt of government aid, nationality and national origin, political affiliation, race, veteran status, and religious beliefs.

A delightful benefit—one that I had not anticipated—accrued to the class from these experiences: After students realized they were not the only classmate in a given social category, they often found themselves emboldened to speak about those experiences publicly in class discussions. The very act of identifying one's self, even anonymously, can be a brave act and can help push a student past that particular social barrier of self-recognition. Identifying themselves publicly was also made easier by knowing that at least some of their classmates could relate to what they were saying, even if they knew they constituted a minority of the class. Just as importantly, classmates who were part of the larger groupings within the class could no longer speak about or on behalf of those in the smaller groupings without being cognizant that they were doing so in the company of classmates who had experience living within those categories. In other words, understanding even a bit of the history and experiences of classmates helped students be more empathetic and less likely to overgeneralize or to claim to speak for a group of which they were not members.

I often tell my classes to interrogate their use of "we," even in a simple sentence. Who is the "we" and whom does it include? Whom does it exclude? Who is erased by its use, and which identities or ideologies are made normative? These are fundamental questions of many of the social sciences, yet many instructors find themselves facing an uphill battle to challenge the presumptions the questions are meant to address. Using clickers to reveal these kinds of differences within the classroom opens up a completely different kind of class discussion, one in which students know from the outset that their own "we" does not make up the totality of their classmates. I observed that classroom discussions quickly became more thoughtful and respectful, with a humility born out of an understanding that one's audience may have more understanding of and experience with the topic at hand than previously assumed.

Before continuing beyond this particular point, two notes of caution: It is not difficult to imagine how this strategy could backfire quite spectacularly. For instance, much of the previous discussion assumes that students discover that they are not alone; what if the questions asked through the clickers display the exact opposite—that a student is indeed the only one with a particular aspect of identity? This could be productive in some circumstances, particularly if that student was assuming that he or she was in the majority and needed the corrective to see that his or her position was more of an outlier than the student realized. But it is far more likely that such an experience would silence an already marginalized student and reduce any potential for that student to speak up publicly. Similarly, identifying social differences anonymously could forge a classroom dynamic wherein students make a game of trying to identify who the outliers are. Such a dynamic could be playful and harmless, but it could also turn vicious and promote rumor mongering.

For both of these reasons, I found it crucial to ensure the questions that I asked through the clickers, particularly those exploring sensitive or controversial terrain, be framed in such a way that students in an extreme minority could be neither identified nor further marginalized by their classmates. Many times, this also meant constructing queries that aggregated some categories that would yield very small minorities in their responses. Given these cautions, however, I believe it is also important to recognize that students who constitute a very small category of any given classroom are often already acutely aware of that status, and in almost every case of which I had personal knowledge, revealing that status to the rest of the class was not a surprise but a relief to the students involved.

Beyond the more generalizable benefits of using clickers across the disciplines, then, my experience has shown that they also allow students to uncover and appreciate social differences within their own classroom, a central learning goal for social science education. Likewise, they allowed the class conversations around controversial and sensitive topics to move beyond clichés and stereotypes into a more in-depth, honest, and respectful dialogue about the impacts of those differences on people's lived experiences and about the substantive disagreements among various students regarding the meaning of those differences. Clickers thus allowed me, as the instructor, to make visible and explicit the ways in which our classroom reflected many of the same social differences as found in broader society. This permitted me to teach social science concepts related to difference and identity more effectively than I would have been able to without the technology. Clickers also allowed me to use the class as a laboratory for exploring less controversial but equally important territory for social science education: survey research.

DECONSTRUCTING SURVEY RESEARCH AND MEDIA REPRESENTATIONS

Survey research methodologies occupy a central role across most of the social science disciplines, particularly those making broadly generalizable claims through large sample sizes. Even disciplines that rely less on large-N methods, such as anthropology, must engage with the power of survey research and media representations of those data in shaping both popular and academic understandings of the social world. Students encountering survey research in the social science classroom often arrive with simplistic notions of how such research is conducted and the surety of the "truth" that the research represents. As a result, deconstructing survey research methodologies— their power and their limitations—becomes a central task of instructors in the social sciences. Media representations of survey research—both public opinion polling conducted by media outlets themselves and more scientific research that is then disseminated through such outlets—further complicate educational efforts while also raising their stakes. Media literacy around research can become one of the most significant benefits of social science education, particularly for those students who do not pursue courses in the social sciences beyond their general education requirements. Here, too, clickers can help.

Clickers transform the social science classroom into a living laboratory where students can experiment with the roles of both researcher and research subject in a low-stakes environment that can yield nearly instant gratification. By experiencing both roles, and by being able to adjust their approaches to asking and responding to survey questions almost instantaneously, students are able to learn about complex methodological challenges through hands-on experience. Although hands-on experimentation with research methods has long been a staple of social science classrooms, the speed with which clickers allow students (and the instructor) to fine-tune their approach to questions and to receive feedback creates a qualitative difference in the educational experience of those experiments.

For example, I will often use clickers to ask students what appear to be, on the surface, basic demographic questions around age, sex, race, and similar categories. As with the previous example around social class, I will then complicate the question in a variety of ways. I may disaggregate what seem like self-evident or binary categories, for instance by adding "other," "neither," and "intersex" to a question about gender, and then discuss the political, ethical, social, and scientific implications of changing the question in that way. Or I may change the wording of the question from "I am . . ." to "I identify as . . . ," again teasing out the implications of the change with the class in open discussion. We also discuss their experiences as respondents to questions in their various iterations, asking things like: "Did you feel more or less included or validated by a particular version of the question? Did you feel confused by the larger number of possible responses? Did you feel like you did not really 'fit in' to any of the categories given as possible responses? Did you find yourself wanting to explain your answer, giving more detail, or nuance, or rationalization?" As a result, students observe a number of phenomena related to survey research.

From the researcher's perspective, students are able to gain insight into how respondents (mis)interpret research questions. They are able to hear from their classmates the multiple ways in which a single question might be understood or misunderstood, even if they themselves understood the question differently. They are better able to consider the ethics of asking questions in more or less inclusive ways. Crucially, they also are able to see how changing a research question—whether the initial query or the potential responses offered—can alter, sometimes profoundly, the results, even with the same group of respondents. Clickers allow instructors to display these common issues in survey research to their students in a much more immediate and visceral way than would be possible by merely discussing the issues, or even experimenting with paper-and-pen surveys.

From the perspective of a survey respondent, students are able to understand the ways in which surveys almost always funnel a broad range of human experience into a relatively limited and narrow set of possible categories in order to quantify and generalize those experiences. My students often responded with frustration in the discussions following a clicker session that "none of the options really fits how I feel about the issue." Exactly! Using that reaction to spur discussions about the limitations of survey research has proven extremely beneficial in advancing student understanding of what surveys are *unable* to tell us as researchers. Paradoxically, it has also improved students' understanding of what surveys *can* tell us: Although students may learn that surveys are significantly more limited in scope than what they had presumed before entering the class, they also gain a more realistic sense of what surveys can do.

In order to drive these lessons home, I have found it extremely useful to allow students as many opportunities as possible to use the clickers to ask their own questions. This occurs in two ways: through student initiation of new clicker questions on the run during a class lecture or discussion and through the use of clickers in student-led facilitations. The first is relatively straightforward and relies primarily on my continual insistence that students are encouraged to offer possible queries for their classmates. Once the pattern is established, students will often respond to a classmate's question or claim by saying, "Let's ask that question with the clickers," and the ease of the technology allows me to set up the question in very little time. I will often phrase the question exactly as the student put it forward initially. Then, with the question displayed on the screen, I will ask the class if the question is worded appropriately to garner the information desired. This gives students a collective opportunity to consider the nuances of the wording and adjust it accordingly. If students disagree on the wording, I will often run the question through the clickers using both versions and then discuss the results and the experience of responding to both questions with the class as a whole. This approach provides students with practice in forming and editing survey questions in a low-stakes manner in nearly every class session, vastly increasing their comfort level and experience in creating relevant, insightful research questions over the course of the term.

My classes often involve student-led facilitations around a particular research topic toward the end of the quarter. As with clicker questions that arise during discussions and lectures, I strongly encourage students to use clickers during their facilitations. However, I ask students to submit the questions to me ahead of time for two reasons: First, it gives me time to set up the questions carefully in collaboration with the students, without the observation of the rest of the class. This more closely mimics a slightly higher-stakes survey process whereby the respondents are seeing a more carefully developed set of questions. Second, vetting the questions ahead of time allows me to avoid the possible pitfalls discussed earlier in this chapter, wherein students are marginalized by participating in a clicker poll that unintentionally isolates their own position, be it ideological, identity based, or otherwise. By developing clicker questions more judiciously during the facilitations they lead, students are able to gain confidence and experience in more carefully considered survey methodology.

I want to emphasize that clicker technology allows this kind of in-class experimentation with survey methods to have a significantly more beneficial impact. Although an instructor could, in theory, replicate each of these steps using other means, including paper-and-pen surveys, the resulting process would of course be much slower. This would mean more time and effort on the part of the instructor, but the more significant, qualitative improvement of clicker technology lies instead in the temporal proximity of each step in the process. By providing students with rapid feedback regarding the ways in which fine-tuning survey questions alters the resulting data, students more readily comprehend and retain the lessons being learned, in terms of both the specific mechanics of particular questions and the larger epistemological questions raised by survey methodologies. Likewise, the greater speeds made possible by clickers allow an instructor to use them much more often. This lowers the stakes of each instance, which also allows students greater experimentation with *failure* as well as success in asking survey questions. I would argue that allowing students to experiment with survey questions that fail to garner the desired information is a crucial step in the process of teaching students to carefully develop successful inquiries.

Although continual experimentation with both creating and responding to survey questions helps students better understand the advantages and limitations of survey research methodologies, clickers also help students better analyze the representations of survey research that appear in media outlets. Throughout the course, I bring in examples of survey research that appear in mass media, and I encourage students to do the same. These examples range from the notoriously inaccurate readers' polls in popular magazines to public opinion and political polling conducted most often by news organizations (sometimes with academic research centers as partners) to comprehensive research results with large sample sizes on a variety of social science research questions reported by media.

Students then replicate the surveys reported in the media with their classmates using the clickers. Past topics from my classes have included favorite characters in currently popular young adult novels to preferred presidential candidates to legalization of marijuana and marriage equality. I find that students, having conducted their own survey research, are consistently much better prepared to analyze the research data generated from these outside sources. Some of the best discussions in the class have come from analyzing classmates' responses to larger, national surveys. Students use the social science concepts they have been learning to postulate why their responses did or did not differ from the large-n samples of national surveys. They discuss the limitations of the surveys, whether the journalistic representations portrayed the research accurately, and how the research might have been improved. We then use the clickers to rate the quality of the research from outside sources. In short, the clickers serve as an effective tool for analysis of media representations of social science research in addition to providing students with experience in shaping their own questions. Thereby, students become not only better amateur social scientists, but also more critically reflective readers of media and therefore better-informed citizens.

CONCLUSION

In addition to its many benefits in any classroom, clicker technology proves particularly useful for teaching some of the crucial concepts in the social sciences. It can be used to undercut students' tendency to think either that all of their classmates agree with them and share similar life experiences or, conversely, that they are isolated in their beliefs and experiences. By polling students regarding their views on controversial topics, clickers are able to reveal the realities of students' lives immediately and confidentially, thus forcing participants to rethink both how they identify themselves and how they identify others. More often than not, this allows students on all sides of an issue to deepen their conversations, making more careful and conscientious arguments rather than taking for granted the correctness or universality of their position.

Clickers also allow instructors to explore the benefits and limits of survey research—how a question is framed, what possible responses are allowed, who is surveyed, and so on—in real and immediate ways. Using the class as a laboratory, instructors can show how modifying a question can drastically alter the results and inferences of a given query. Students can also experiment with their own questions, either on the spot or in student facilitations. Because survey research is a methodology on which much social science and public opinion research depends, using clickers to foster a critical examination of survey methods becomes an invaluable tool for instruction while also increasing literacy regarding the ways in which social science research is presented through media outlets. As such, clickers provide students with a roadmap to confronting their own inconvenient facts—whether generated by social science research or other sources—from a position more nuanced and informed than the common defaults of blind acceptance or cynical rejection.

5

Using Clickers in Science, Technology, Engineering, and Mathematics

Robyn E. Goacher, Danyelle Moore, Luis Sanchez,
Paul R. Schupp, and Yonghong Tong

Teaching in science, technology, engineering, and mathematics (STEM) fields is challenging because of the combination of high content levels and specialized vocabulary that students have to learn to participate in class and complete assignments. Instructors in STEM classrooms might find it difficult to cover all the content while engaging students in active learning. STEM instructors must therefore be open to using new tools and techniques, such as classroom clickers, to help them achieve learning goals and enhance student performance in a flexible and efficient way.

In 2009, the Center for the Advancement of Scholarship, Teaching, and Learning (CASTL) introduced clickers to instructors at Niagara University (NU), a small liberal arts college in Western New York. CASTL offered training on an as-needed basis, focusing on technical skills and encouraging exploration. The instructors began experimenting with clickers and incorporating them into lessons to see what did and did not work and whether clickers were worth their time and effort. Of the 163 faculty members at NU, 21 currently use clickers in their instruction. Of the current users, 7 are STEM faculty. NU's clicker collection has grown to include more than 300 handheld clicker transmitters coordinated through CASTL.

Finding clickers to be useful, flexible instructional tools worth the time and effort, we have recently begun to share our experiences with one another and compare our experiences with the literature. The techniques discussed here typically help STEM instructors achieve two important goals: facilitating the teaching and learning of content and eliciting student feedback to evaluate teaching and learning. In this chapter, we share our experiences and offer advice to other STEM and non-STEM instructors who are considering using clickers.

We have found clickers to have several potential benefits in STEM courses. They can

- allow instructors to check for student understanding by asking questions before introducing new content, periodically throughout lessons, and after instruction;
- help stimulate participation when used to start discussions, pose provocative questions, or overcome student reluctance to participate;
- provide convenience for instructors when administering quizzes and serve as an often-preferred mode of testing for students;
- help guide instructional direction by providing data about areas in which students are and are not having difficulty, so that lessons can be adjusted in real time;
- facilitate instructors' administration of informal student perception surveys to receive feedback on courses during the semester, using them as "in-slips" (required for entry to the classroom) or "out-slips" (required prior to leaving at the end of a class period); and
- enable students to anonymously grade peer projects.

Throughout this chapter, we describe how much time teaching with clickers takes, the value gained from use, and specific examples of how we use clickers.

THE LITERATURE

After using clickers for several years, the authors are pleased to find that the clicker literature in STEM supports the effectiveness of these devices, even in content-heavy courses where instructors often question whether a pedagogical intervention is worth the time. We believe that, in the case of clickers, the answer is "frequently, yes!"

Each of this chapter's authors began experimenting with clickers independently and have personally discovered a number of preferred techniques in his or her STEM courses, all before reviewing much of the published literature. However, excellent literature resources about clickers in STEM are growing. Of particular note is the online database maintained by Derek Bruff, director of the Vanderbilt Center for Teaching at Vanderbilt University, which had indexed almost 300 clicker-related references in many STEM and non-STEM disciplines as of March 25, 2014 (Bruff, 2014). It is instructive to see that other STEM instructors report positive experiences that align with our experiences that clickers are flexible, effective tools with which to facilitate active learning (Gachago, 2008; Maguire & Maguire, 2013). Many publications have further revealed satisfyingly positive attitudes from students and instructors who observe that the use of clickers makes their classes come "alive as never before" (Kaleta & Joosten, 2007).

Because clickers are a classroom response system, instructors typically use them in the classroom to engage students in class-wide and small-group discussion, thus fostering active learning, helping evaluate student learning, and providing a better understanding of how students learn in class (Bruff, 2009). Engineering instructors with large classes have reported that teaching with clickers improves students' grasp of engineering concepts and supports active learning through discussion (Boyle & Nicol, 2003). This interaction helps instructors alleviate their concerns about weak conceptual understanding, insufficient interaction and discussion, and low motivation. These published reports suggest that STEM instructors are likely to find that classroom clicker use is worth the time and effort to enhance student learning.

Clickers and Student Performance

Although it is well established that clickers have *perceived* benefits, it is less clear how clickers change student learning and performance on tests (Camacho-Miñano & del Campo, 2014). Some have reported increased grades (Poirier & Feldman, 2007; Rush et al., 2013), but it is unclear whether the effects are significant. Shapiro and Gordon (2012) found that clicker use improved student *fact retention* considerably (10%–13%). Others have reported that the in-class use of clickers improves the performance on examinations of only the highest-achieving students (Addison, Wright, & Milner, 2009) or that clickers do not significantly affect grades (Hecht, Adams, Cunningham, Lane, & Howell, 2013; Sutherlin, Sutherlin, & Akpanudo, 2013; Welch, 2013). For situations in which no effects are observed, some have suggested that the value of active learning might overshadow the benefit of using clickers (Martyn, 2007). The effects may be rather subtle in certain cases in which active learning was used prior to the implementation of clickers (Crossgrove & Curran, 2008). Some of the uncertainty regarding clicker efficacy may be due to the fact that clicker use in science classes, such as chemistry, is still at the early adoption stage (Emenike & Holme, 2012). As clicker use expands, we expect that the literature will provide a more complete picture of the effects on student test scores (Sutherlin et al., 2013). We are aware of no reports in which clickers were shown to hurt student performance, and it appears that as a tool that promotes active learning, they can improve grades if appropriately used.

Clickers and Social Factors

The diversity of student backgrounds in STEM courses can be quite high. Clicker activities can be an efficient way to benefit all students, including ethnic minorities, students from other cultures, and female students who might be more vulnerable to low participation (Lopez, Nandagopal, Shavelson, Szu, & Penn, 2013). Social factors may impact successful clicker use more than technological factors (Trees & Jackson, 2007). Students are the ones who must accept the technology to positively affect their learning. The role of instructors is to judiciously assess whether their classroom is appropriate for clickers. Using clickers "for the sake of it" is not welcomed by students (Caldwell, 2007), especially when technical issues cause delays or when students have to pay for the devices (Graham, Tripp, Seawright, & Joeckel, 2007).

Clickers as a Tool for Active Learning and Peer Instruction

Recent meta-analysis of STEM pedagogy literature clearly supports active-learning approaches (Freeman et al., 2014). Clickers may help facilitate more active-learning approaches and increase student performance (Blasco-Arcas, Buil, Hernandex-Ortega, & Sese, 2013), and active learning appears to be more advantageous than traditional lectures (Trees & Jackson, 2007). The decision making required by answering questions, made manageable by clicker technology, is one way to incorporate active learning in STEM classrooms of varying size. Clickers may also be integrated as tools for managing favorable pedagogical methods such as Mazur's peer instruction (PI), originally introduced in physics courses (Crouch & Mazur, 2001; Mazur, 1997), and Michaelsen's team-based learning (TBL), introduced in medical instruction (Michaelsen, 1983). Clickers are not essential to PI or TBL, but can facilitate and enhance PI (Mazur, 2009) and TBL (Pileggi & O'Neill, 2008) activities. Implementation of PI using clickers has been successful in other areas, such as biology (Smith, Wood, Krauter, & Knight, 2011) and computer science (Zingaro & Porter, 2014).

Using clickers without a plan will likely not improve teaching, enhance student learning, or advance STEM pedagogy more generally (Chen & Lan, 2013; Landrum, 2013). Instructors should be creative when designing real-time, active-learning exercises using clickers and should share these experiences with their colleagues. As Lantz (2010) observed, "Clickers can be used in the classroom as an amusing novelty, without taking advantage of cognitive principles that enhance learning. However, clickers may best be used by following cognitive principles that will aid students' understanding and memory of material" (p. 556).

Fortunately, recent literature has provided many promising examples in which clickers have been used very creatively in combination with other pedagogical methods to teach important topics in biology (Brewer & Gardner, 2013), economics (Bostian & Holt, 2013), and chemistry (Ryan, 2013). Other interesting clicker-focused studies have permitted the direct measurement of students' attention during class (Bunce, Flens, & Neiles, 2010) and the assessment of the disparities between students' perception of knowledge and actual proficiency with scientific literature (Bandyopadhyay, 2013).

CLICKERS GUIDING INSTRUCTIONAL DIRECTION

STEM instructors typically love data. Part of the joy of instructing with clickers is the data provided by the responses and the choice of what to do with this information. As STEM instructors, we use clickers for hard content—"What do you know?" (see the "Teaching Content" section)—and to elicit feedback—"How's this going for you?" (see the "Clickers for Fielding Student Feedback" section).

In all applications, the instructor chooses what to do with the information collected. This depends on the instructor's interest and style. Sometimes we use clickers to start a class discussion and never return to the data. The information serves its purpose in the moment. Sometimes we return to clicker data after a class session to look for trends in missed questions in order to address the topics in a different way during the next class or to identify and reach out to struggling students.

One of the best advantages of using clickers to teach content in any discipline is the option for instructors to use the data to adjust their teaching in real time. Clicker questions serve as no- or low-credit formative assessments that give instructors valuable information about student knowledge. In some of our most active class sessions, up to half of the class time is occupied by students answering clicker questions, with confirmations, explanations, and clarifications of varying length interspersed between questions. Student understanding is checked and found to be sufficient (move on) or deficient (clarify the topic).

Feedback collected via clickers also offers students an opportunity to express thoughts and ideas about the instructor's teaching, pace, and clarity. Yonghong Tong's computer science course is a good example of how clickers help instructors evaluate pacing and ensure students have the requisite background. Before he used clickers in his courses, Tong's students seldom expressed their thoughts about teaching pace even though he frequently invited them to give such feedback. The only way to determine whether the class was well paced and not too difficult, therefore, was to interpret quiz and exam performance. Clickers give him a more valid indicator of how well lessons are paced and how well students comprehend. Asking questions early in the semester allows instructors time to adjust. For example, in Tong's mobile app development course, students were deficient in needed programming skills, so he added this content into his lessons.

TEACHING CONTENT

We use clickers to check student knowledge, administer graded quizzes, promote stimulating discussions through conversation starters, pose provocative questions to engage students, and overcome student reluctance to participate in class. Clickers are tools with which to quickly and efficiently collect data from students. Instructors can then use this information productively for the majority of the class period, which can have a great impact in teaching (Anderson, Healy, Kole, & Bourne Jr., 2013).

Checking Knowledge

Instructors must understand what they should teach, what knowledge students already have, and what knowledge students need to acquire. Clicker questions can help gauge student knowledge, helping instructors teach to promote student understanding, encourage creative thinking, and develop critical thinking and inquiry. MacArthur (2013) and others have suggested that educators should focus on understanding what goes on during clicker activities rather than conducting studies in which clicker use is the only factor being examined.

Several of us use clicker questions to check students' pre-existing content knowledge. Prior to a structured lesson segment, or "lecture" in which we teach material, we ask students about definitions or relationships between ideas or ask them to perform a mathematical calculation. Students' performance on pre-check questions help guide how time is spent in lecture. Often, intentionally or not, clicker questions spark discussions about common misconceptions or mistakes. Our clicker use is not limited to assessment of prior knowledge. In chemistry class sessions, Robyn Goacher often warms up the class with a few clicker questions and then intersperses clicker questions with instructional slides, using the questions to check understanding and provide practice in making decisions and calculations using the concepts just learned. Asking "Are you with me?" questions is, in fact, among the most common uses of clickers (Salemi, 2009). In a similar manner, Luis Sanchez uses clicker questions for intense, pre-exam review sessions, specifically to help students identify their weaknesses in certain topics. Recent studies have suggested that clicker activities in which students review content in a gamelike manner may have a significant impact on long-term content retention (Crossgrove & Curran, 2008; Rush et al., 2013).

What Questions? How Often?

In our experience, clicker questions are best used to make decisions or select the best (not always the sole "right") answer from a few options (multiple-choice questions) and short mathematical questions (numerical entry). Although this may seem limiting, there is a wide variety of questions that can be probed with these formats. Uses range from the introduction of new points, perhaps in the form of brain teasers (Wagner, 2009), to the identification at the end of class of what students consider to be the "muddiest point" (Angelo & Cross, 1993), allowing the difficult areas to be reviewed in the next lecture (King, 2011).

Although multiple-choice questions are easy to administer with clickers, instructors widely recognize that such questions can be difficult to write (Bruff, 2009). We have found that writing effective clicker questions can be challenging and requires some trial and error. However, as clickers have become recognized tools for active learning, databases and books have been written with questions for STEM education. The National Science Foundation (NSF) maintains a library of more than 2,000 multiple-choice mathematics questions designed for classroom voting (Cline, 2012). ConcepTests, originally developed by Eric Mazur for physics but now available on the World Wide Web for several STEM disciplines, and the Cornell GoodQuestions project (www.math.cornell.edu/~GoodQuestions) are also helpful resources. The NSF database contains information about whether specific questions are appropriate for quick checks of information, which most students answer correctly, or are common-error "trick" questions, or are questions to provoke discussion. Discipline-specific resources are also published in print journals and online.

Some multiple-choice questions are too superficial, because they allow students to simply compare the given options instead of rationally thinking of the solution. In these cases, free answer through text entry is preferable, but can be more technically challenging depending on the clicker technology employed.

We have not found clickers to be effective for all STEM teaching applications because of the limited question and response formats. For example, clickers appear to have limited effectiveness for drawing molecules in organic chemistry, programming code in computer science, reporting mathematical results for long logical problems, and solving multistep mathematical problems. We have also found that clickers do not fully work for the sustained instruction of topics that are highly complex or visual or that involve a great deal of discussion. Instead, for these topics, we have found that clickers are best used for stimulating discussion instead of as a means of presenting or assessing content.

Fortunately, we have found workarounds for approaching difficult STEM teaching situations. For instance, in organic chemistry, where drawing molecules is essential, some authors have found that using numbers to label atoms and bonds in the molecular structures allows the design of on-screen questions that can be answered via numerical input (Flynn, 2011). For complex situations, such as describing organic reaction mechanisms, well-designed questions permit the submission of answers using letters and numbers (Straumanis & Ruder, 2009). Clicker questions can be adjusted for many pedagogical purposes, including asking two-stage questions, in which students first answer a content question and then answer a question about why they chose their answer, allowing for self-reflection and examination of what students know and how (Chandrasegaran, Treagust, & Mocerino, 2007; Wagner, 2009). We expect to see further developments for complex clicker questions as more research is published and as technology advances.

Teaching with clickers should serve the class learning goals; the class should not serve clickers. Student learning must be first priority. Instructors should avoid clicker overload, which may lower student enthusiasm (Reay, Li, & Bao, 2008) and accept that clickers may be ill suited to some tasks. None of us uses clickers in every class. In fact, our students enjoy the mystery of whether a given class session will include clickers. Clicker questions do take time, as the students must process their decisions. Thus, a balance must be struck between delivering content and clarifying content through lecture and engaging in clicker activities. For content-heavy classes, clickers are therefore more amenable when used in a "flipped" classroom or when clicker results guide instructional emphasis in class and student studying outside of class. Even with these approaches, Robyn Goacher used clickers in 40%–60% of the meetings of her analytical chemistry class, a course that is ideal for clickers because it involves many fundamental concepts and algebraic computations. For more open-ended, seminar-style discussion (e.g., environmental chemistry), she used clickers in 15%–20% of class sessions.

Because some students solve questions faster than others, we risk introducing unproductive time with numerous clicker questions. The time management concern can be mitigated by asking simpler, shorter questions, by giving an "I have no idea" answer option, by adding a timer to the question slides, by using self-paced polling, by asking students to negotiate questions in pairs or groups if they are not answering quickly enough, and by giving students extension work to take a topic further while others finish the clicker question.

Graded Clicker Quizzes

The quiz: a hated but helpful demon! Quizzes check student understanding and help ensure that students are ready to move on or be more formally tested with a form of summative assessment. Clicker quizzes can make life easier on everyone. For the instructor, clicker quizzes are scored by the software. For the student, the quiz is done in real time, and the instructor provides immediate feedback on their performance and clarifies answers. Immediate feedback is of high importance for the effectiveness of clicker activities (Lantz & Stawiski, 2014).

Clicker quizzes can be administered to individuals or to teams, and questions may be asked all at once or interspersed with lecture and other activities. The goal is to evaluate students' knowledge in a way that motivates studying by assigning points for correctness. Maguire and Maguire (2013) used clickers in a computer science course in team-based learning, with 20% of the course grade resulting from quiz responses. Their research showed that clicker use enhanced attendance, attention, and engagement.

Some of us use clickers for reading quizzes in order to motivate students to read the assigned text before class and respond to important concepts. A small portion of the course grade, typically 5% or less, is assigned as incentive to take clicker reading quizzes seriously. Recent studies have shown greater effects in student learning when clicker questions were tied to course credit (Jones, Crandal, Vogler, & Robinson, 2013), but it is also advisable not to improperly reward students for trivial accomplishments (White, Syncox, & Alters, 2011).

Stimulating Discussion

Although instructors often desire regular, meaningful classroom discussions, we can struggle to create them. As instructors, we ask difficult or controversial questions of our students to get them thinking. Appropriate instructor-guided, clicker-initiated discussion, however, can help students understand STEM concepts (Knight, Wise & Southard, 2013). In our experience, clicker questions can spark conversation at any point during a class session. Sometimes these questions serve as the stimulus for a predetermined lecture, and other times they set the direction for more open-ended class discussion.

In courses with more right/wrong and mathematical concepts, clicker questions can also stimulate discussion and help go beyond routine "plug-and-chug," whereby students simply plug different numbers into set formulas without considering why they are doing so. Multiple-choice questions can include common-error answers, which identify misconceptions or pitfalls in the process or concept being taught. Open-ended numerical entry questions can reveal differing results in student calculations. Showing the response plots after asking a tricky question can be very revealing. When students choose a popular wrong answer, their misconception is immediately identified, and, together with the instructor, they can examine why their reasoning is incorrect or what tricky step they missed in a calculation. The anonymous nature of clickers allows for full class participation, because it mitigates the fear or shame associated with giving a wrong answer publically.

We handle the response plots in several ways. Following the team-based learning or peer instruction approach, students may actively reason out the counterargument to the misconception in pairs or small groups. Alternatively, the instructor can directly clarify the point and give students a minute to summarize the argument in their own words, structuring a few minutes of note making into class. We suggest that when individuals (or the whole class) answer a tricky question correctly, instructors ask students to pause and identify what step in their logic or mathematical operations would be the most likely to trip them up on a future test or application. This kind of metacognition helps students learn not only the concepts, but also how best to *learn.*

The mere act of answering clicker questions requires all students to form an opinion, and they are then more likely to engage in class discussion instead of allowing a few students to dominate the discussion (Cline, 2006). Using student responses as the basis for class discussion is the foundation of Mazur's peer instruction approach (Watkins & Mazur, 2013).

As Albert Einstein said, "Imagination is more important than knowledge." In computer programming classes, imagination is critical, because there are always alternative solutions to a real-life problem. Students and instructors work together to perform brainstorming in computer science courses in which mathematics, technology, and art are integrated.

In Yonghong Tong's computer science class, students work in assigned groups of three or four to (a) read a multiple-choice question, (b) brainstorm and discuss as a group, (c) respond by clicker as a group, and (d) discuss and explain results to one another. Because all students answer simultaneously, the class sees diverse answers rather than groups agreeing to a first group's suggestion in open whole-class discussion. Furthermore, students in Tong's mobile app development class have expressed interest in developing their own mobile clicker app, which is the result of their positive experience using clickers in class. Using classroom technology may stimulate students in STEM, especially in technology and engineering, to design and create their own technical innovations.

CLICKERS FOR FIELDING STUDENT FEEDBACK

The anonymity of clickers makes them very useful for eliciting feedback, which allows STEM instructors to evaluate student learning and their teaching efficacy. Instructors can administer informal student perception surveys with which to evaluate courses during the semester, using them as either in-slips or out-slips. Clickers are also ideal for allowing students to anonymously grade peer projects.

Taking the Classroom "Temperature" and Informal Student Perception Surveys

At NU, we have no official midterm course evaluations, so clickers offer instructors a way to collect and analyze anonymous statistics on class progress. Official evaluations of 15 or more questions may take 10–15 minutes of class time, but survey collection in class guarantees high response rates. If the classroom environment is comfortable enough, displaying the opinion graphs after voting can also invite follow-up discussion or comments on written slips of paper.

Robyn Goacher has found clickers to be useful for such informal midterm course evaluations as well as for routine, short "in-slips" and "out-slips" consisting of one or two questions that take a minute to answer. These clicker questions are designed to "take the temperature" of the classroom and assess how the course is going. In-slip or class-starter questions include questions like "How deeply did you read the chapter?" "How well did you understand the reading?" "Did you have a good weekend?" or "How do you feel class pace is so far?" Options for student responses can then be set up with a Likert scale or using more descriptive (and occasionally humorous) multiple-choice answers. On a purely logistical level, in-slip questions allow the instructor to check that all clicker responses register properly. Second, real-time statistics on students' perceived preparation level help the instructor choose how to scaffold material and provide structure for discussion about study habits or course expectations. Out-slip clicker questions like "How clear was today's content to you?" or "Which of the following topics from today's class do you need to focus your studies on?" help students reflect on the course session.

These informal student surveys are easily made anonymous, either through software settings or by asking students to scramble clickers. Importantly, by enabling instructors to ask students for opinions, clicker surveys send a message to students that they matter. Their thoughts are valuable to the instructor and will influence how the class is run. This enhances the construction of a safe, community-centered classroom where all voices are respected. Also, as Salemi (2009) noted, using clickers increases the abundance of student-originated questions in class, partly due to their confidence that the instructor values their views.

Anonymous Evaluation of Peer Projects

Several of us have used clickers to collect student opinions on other students' performance on class presentations, group projects, and so on. Always anonymous to their peers, and sometimes anonymous to the instructor, these survey questions may ask students about their teammates' contributions in group work or about the quality of work produced by other students. In our experience, clicker voting/grading of peer projects can provide an upbeat form of student feedback. However, administering peer evaluations by clicker does not remove the concern that students tend to award their classmates with high marks. Thus, clear rules and scoring rubrics for peer evaluations must be used.

Clicker peer evaluations can be easy and rapid. For example, Luis Sanchez used clickers for peer grading during a presentation session for 57 students organized into 14 teams. The students evaluated each other's presentations considering five criterion statements: (a) The topic was well introduced, (b) the presenters demonstrated knowledge of the topic, (c) the presentation was well organized, (d) the speakers presented the material clearly, and (e) the audience learned something new. Using a Likert scale from *strongly disagree* (1) to *strongly agree* (5), scores on these five criteria were submitted simultaneously—for instance, "5, 3, 4, 4, 5." It took a couple of minutes to practice entering feedback, and only one student did it incorrectly. Afterward, students were able to individually rate each subsequent presentation within one minute for all five criteria. The instructor then easily exported the data to a spreadsheet to generate "audience grades." Gathering the same information using paper forms would have required almost 800 forms and several hours to transcribe the responses into usable data. This case exemplifies how instructors can achieve efficiency by using clickers to collect large amounts of information.

"I LOVE CLICKERS": STEM STUDENTS' THOUGHTS ABOUT CLICKERS

One of our informal chemistry course surveys asked students what they thought of class sessions (lecture, discussion) as well as quizzes (clicker and written). For class sessions, several students referred to clickers: "My favorite thing about this class is using the clickers to make lectures interactive"; "[Add] more clicker questions, helps me feel engaged and interested"; and "I love clickers!" In regard to clicker quizzes, responses included: "[I] liked clicker quizzes"; "[Add] more clicker quizzes, reading quizzes are always a good motivational tool"; and "Explanations given after the answer was given were very helpful." Student enthusiasm for clickers have been reported to be as high as 100% in mathematics (Popelka, 2010) and 90% for undergraduate economics (Salemi, 2009). Anecdotally, in our own classes and in others (e.g., Cline, 2006), clicker questions make class seem to "go faster" and are fun for students.

CONCLUSION

STEM instructors should consider the potential improvement in classroom dynamics that typically accompanies the implementation of clickers. A recent study of more than 1,500 chemistry instructors found that 18.6% use clickers (Emenike & Holme, 2012). We welcomed clickers into our classrooms at NU and will continue their use. Clickers are simple to operate, easy to incorporate, versatile in their applications, and appropriate for achieving STEM instructional goals. Clickers offer a flexible and effective tool for teaching in a variety of STEM subjects. Indeed, our most significant challenge in clicker implementation has been availability of the devices on campus, as interest grows faster than the number of available clickers.

Requiring students to purchase their own devices may limit the number of instructors willing to try clickers in their classroom. At NU, students are not required to purchase clickers, because the institution has a stock of well-maintained sets. We believe this approach supports a positive attitude toward clickers and helps the institution overcome some logistical problems related to student-owned devices, such as students forgetting to recharge them or bring them to class (Graham et al., 2007).

Our university purchased Turning Technologies devices. But others are available, and there is no need to limit clicker use to just one device. No two classes are the same, and the diversity of clicker applications in STEM classrooms is remarkable. We hope STEM teachers will not allow minor logistical challenges or clickers' novelty to deter them from experimenting with clickers and experiencing how useful they can be.

REFERENCES

Addison, S., Wright, A., & Milner, R. (2009). Using clickers to improve student engagement and performance in an introductory biochemistry class. *Biochemistry and Molecular Biology Education, 37*(2), 84–91.

Anderson, L. S., Healy, A. F., Kole, J. A., & Bourne Jr., L. E. (2013). The clicker technique: Cultivating efficient teaching and successful learning. *Applied Cognitive Psychology, 27*(2), 222–234.

Angelo, T. A., & Cross, K. P. (1993). *Classroom assessment techniques: A handbook for college teachers* (2nd ed.). San Francisco, CA: Jossey-Bass.

Bandyopadhyay, A. (2013). Measuring the disparities between biology undergraduates' perceptions and their actual knowledge of scientific literature with clickers. *Journal of Academic Librarianship, 39*(2), 194–201.

Blasco-Arcas, L., Buil, I., Hernandex-Ortega, B., & Sese, F. J. (2013). Using clickers in class: The role of interactivity, active collaborative learning and engagement in learning performance. *Computers & Education, 62*, 102–110.

Bostian, A. J. A., & Holt, C. A. (2013). Veconlab classroom clicker games: The wisdom of crowds and the winner's curse. *Journal of Economic Education, 44*(3), 217–229.

Boyle, J. T., & Nicol, D. J. (2003). Using classroom communication systems to support interaction and discussion in large class settings. *Research in Learning Technology, 11*(3), 43–57.

Brewer, M. S., & Gardner, G. E. (2013). Teaching evolution through the Hardy-Weinberg principle: A real-time, active-learning exercise using classroom response devices. *American Biology Teacher, 75*(7), 476–479.

Bruff, D. (2009). *Teaching with classroom response systems: Creating active learning environments.* San Francisco, CA: Jossey-Bass.

Bruff, D. (2014). *Classroom response system ("clickers") bibliography. Retrieved June 11, 2014,* from http://cft.vanderbilt.edu/docs/classroom-response-system-clickers-bibliography/

Bunce, D. M., Flens, E. A., & Neiles, K. Y. (2010). How long can students pay attention in class? A study of student attention decline using clickers. *Journal of Chemical Education, 87*(12), 1438–1443.

Caldwell, J. E. (2007). Clickers in the large classroom: Current research and best-practice tips. *CBE-Life Sciences Education, 6*(1), 9–20.

Camacho-Miñano, M., & del Campo, C. (2014). Useful interactive teaching tool for learning: Clickers in higher education. *Interactive Learning Environments,* (ahead of print), 1–18. doi: 10.1080/10494820.2014.917108

Chandrasegaran, A. L., Treagust, D. F., & Mocerino, M. (2007). The development of a two-tier multiple-choice diagnostic instrument for evaluating secondary school students' ability to describe and explain chemical reactions using multiple levels of representation. *Chemistry Education Research and Practice, 8*(3), 293–307.

Chen, T.-L., & Lan, Y.-L. (2013). Using a personal response system as an in-class assessment tool in the teaching of basic college chemistry. *Australasian Journal of Educational Technology, 29*(1), 32–40.

Cline, K. S. (2006). Classroom voting in mathematics. *Mathematics Teacher, 100*(2), 100–104.

Cline, K. S. (2012). A question library for classroom voting. *Mathematics Teacher, 106*(3), 212–218.

Crossgrove, K., & Curran, K. L. (2008). Using clickers in nonmajors- and majors-level biology courses: Student opinion, learning, and long-term retention of course material. *CBE-Life Sciences Education, 7*(1), 146–154.

Crouch, C. H., & Mazur, E. (2001). Peer instruction: Ten years of experience and results. *American Journal of Physics, 69*(9), 970–977.

Emenike, M. E., & Holme, T. A. (2012). Classroom response systems have not "crossed the chasm'": Estimating numbers of chemistry faculty who use clickers. *Journal of Chemical Education, 89*(4), 465–469.

Flynn, A. B. (2011). Developing problem-solving skills through retrosynthetic analysis and clickers in organic chemistry. *Journal of Chemical Education, 88*(11), 1496–1500.

Freeman, S., Eddy, S. L., McDonough, M., Smith, M. K., Okoroafor, N., Jordt, H., & Wenderoth, M. P. (2014). Active learning increases student performance in science, engineering, and mathematics. *Proceedings of the National Academy of Sciences.* doi: 10.1073/pnas.1319030111

Gachago, D. (2008). *Feedback on personal response systems ("clickers")—lecturers' perspective.* Retrieved May 28, 2014, from http://www.scieng.ed.ac.uk/LTStrategy/resources/Clicker_feedback_v0_7_incl_exec_summary.pdf

Graham, C. R., Tripp, T. R., Seawright, L., & Joeckel, G. I. (2007). Empowering or compelling reluctant participators using audience response systems. *Active Learning in Higher Education, 8*(3), 233–258.

Hecht, S., Adams, W. H., Cunningham, M. A., Lane, I. F., & Howell, N. E. (2013). Student performance and course evaluations before and after use of the classroom performance system™ in a third-year veterinary radiology course. *Veterinary Radiology & Ultrasound, 54*(2), 114–121.

Jones, S. J., Crandal, J., Vogler, J. S., & Robinson, D. H. (2013). Classroom response systems facilitate student accountability, readiness, and learning. *Journal of Educational Computing Research, 49*(2), 155–171.

Kaleta, R., & Joosten, T. (2007). Student response systems: A University of Wisconsin System study of clickers. *EDUCAUSE ECAR Bulletin, 2007*(10), 1–12.

King, D. B. (2011). Using clickers to identify the muddiest points in large chemistry classes. *Journal of Chemical Education, 88*(11), 1485–1488.

Knight, J. K., Wise, S. B., & Southard, K. M. (2013). Understanding clicker discussions: Student reasoning and the impact of instructional cues. *CBE-Life Sciences Education, 12*(4), 645–654.

Landrum, R. E. (2013). The ubiquitous clicker: SoTL applications for scientist–educators. *Teaching of Psychology, 40*(2), 98–103.

Lantz, M. E. (2010). The use of "clickers" in the classroom: Teaching innovation or merely an amusing novelty? *Computers in Human Behavior, 26*(4), 556–561.

Lantz, M. E., & Stawiski, A. (2014). Effectiveness of clickers: Effect of feedback and the timing of questions on learning. *Computers in Human Behavior, 31*, 280–286.

Lopez, E. J., Nandagopal, K., Shavelson, R. J., Szu, E., & Penn, J. (2013). Self-regulated learning study strategies and academic performance in undergraduate organic chemistry: An investigation examining ethnically diverse students. *Journal of Research in Science Teaching, 50*(6), 660–676.

MacArthur, J. (2013). How will classroom response systems "cross the chasm"? *Journal of Chemical Education, 90*(3), 273–275.

Maguire, P., & Maguire, R. (2013). Can clickers enhance team based learning? Findings from a computer science module. *All Ireland Journal of Teaching and Learning in Higher Education, 5*(3), 142 1 – 142 17.

Martyn, M. (2007). Clickers in the classroom: An active learning approach. *EDUCAUSE Quarterly, 30*(2), 71–74.

Mazur, E. (1997). *Peer instruction: A user's manual.* Upper Saddle River, NJ: Prentice Hall.

Mazur, E. (2009). Farewell, lecture? *Science, 323*(5910), 50–51.

Michaelsen, L. K. (1983). Team learning in large classes. *New Directions for Teaching and Learning, 1983*(14), 13–22.

Pileggi, R., & O'Neill, P. N. (2008). Team-based learning using an audience response system: An innovative method of teaching diagnosis to undergraduate dental students. *Journal of Dental Education, 72*(10), 1182–1188.

Poirier, C. R., & Feldman, R. S. (2007). Promoting active learning using individual response technology in large introductory psychology classes. *Teaching of Psychology, 34*(3), 194–196.

Popelka, S. R. (2010). Now we're really CLICKING! *Mathematics Teacher, 104*(4), 290–295.

Reay, N. W., Li, P., & Bao, L. (2008). Testing a new voting machine question methodology. *American Journal of Physics, 76*(2), 171–178.

Rush, B. R., White, B. J., Allbaugh, R. A., Jones, M. L., Klocke, E. E., Miesner, M., . . . & Roush, J. K. (2013). Investigation into the impact of audience response devices on short- and long-term content retention. *Journal of Veterinary Medical Education, 40*(2), 171–176.

Ryan, B. J. (2013). Line up, line up: Using technology to align and enhance peer learning and assessment in a student centred foundation organic chemistry module. *Chemistry Education Research and Practice, 14*(3), 229–238.

Salemi, M. K. (2009). Clickenomics: Using a classroom response system to increase student engagement in a large-enrollment principles of economics course. *Journal of Economic Education, 40*(4), 385–404.

Shapiro, A. M., & Gordon, L. T. (2012). A controlled study of clicker-assisted memory enhancement in college classrooms. *Applied Cognitive Psychology, 26*(4), 635–643.

Smith, M. K., Wood, W. B., Krauter, K., & Knight, J. K. (2011). Combining peer discussion with instructor explanation increases student learning from in-class concept questions. *CBE-Life Sciences Education, 10*(1), 55–63.

Straumanis, A. R., & Ruder, S. M. (2009). New bouncing curved arrow technique for the depiction of organic mechanisms. *Journal of Chemical Education, 86*(12), 1389–1391.

Sutherlin, A. L., Sutherlin, G. R., & Akpanudo, U. M. (2013). The effect of clickers in university science courses. *Journal of Science Education and Technology, 22*(5), 651–666.

Trees, A. R., & Jackson, M. H. (2007). The learning environment in clicker classrooms: Student processes of learning and involvement in large university-level courses using student response systems. *Learning, Media and Technology, 32*(1), 21–40.

Wagner, B. D. (2009). A variation on the use of interactive anonymous quizzes in the chemistry classroom. *Journal of Chemical Education, 86*(11), 1300–1303.

Watkins, J., & Mazur, E. (2013). Retaining students in science, technology, engineering, and mathematics (STEM) majors. *Journal of College Science Teaching, 42*, 36–41.

Welch, S. (2013). Effectiveness of classroom response systems within an active learning environment. *Journal of Nursing Education, 52*(11), 653–656.

White, P. D., Syncox, D., & Alters, B. (2011). Clicking for grades? Really? Investigating the use of clickers for awarding grade-points in post-secondary education. *Interactive Learning Environments, 19*(5), 551–561.

Zingaro, D., & Porter, L. (2014). Peer instruction in computing: The value of instructor intervention. *Computers & Education, 71*, 87–96.

6

Making Biostatistics "Click"

Paul S. Weiss

Some of the most interesting classes we take in college are those in which the professor finds some way to illustrate a complex theoretical idea with a demonstration. I remember watching my physics professor pull a pendulum—resting on a makeshift pedestal—up to his chin and let it go. I am sure I was not the only one in the class who was expecting to see my professor laid out on his back when the pendulum made its return. He flinched a little but remained unscathed from the experiment. I liked science before, but after the demonstration I was a huge fan, and it shaped the way I teach my own students. When it comes to teaching biostatistics, I find it really helps to have some way to show the students that these concepts and methods really work.

When the opportunity to use clickers in class presented itself, I jumped at the chance to try them out. The allure for me was the opportunity for students to be able to enter alphanumeric information into the clicker. Now, I can ask students to work out a problem in class and enter their answer, rounded to a fixed number of decimal points, into the device. This is particularly nice for a host of reasons. Consider a simple in-class exercise where I provide a small sample of values and ask the students to calculate the standard deviation. Here are some data:

2   3   3   5   7   11   18   20   21

Calculating the standard deviation can be accomplished easily by entering the values into a scientific calculator with statistical functions, but, for the sake of argument, let's say we have to do this by hand. At this point, the students have to follow a fairly complicated set of directions: They have to find the mean, subtract it from each of the observations, square those deviations, and sum them up. Then they have to divide that sum by a nonintuitive value and finish up by taking the square root. When I ask the students to report the standard deviation to two decimal places for this sample, I expect to see a diverse set of answers. Before clickers, I would be limited to asking, "Who got an answer of 7.76?" A show of hands around the room would tell me who got the correct answer, but I would have no idea what went wrong for the rest of the class. Adding clickers to the mix gives me a much different avenue to measure success. When I call up the results from the clickers, I might see something like this:

7.76	80%
60.25	5%
7.762087	4%
7.318166	4%
7.32	3%
53.56	2%
0	2%

First, when students enter an answer with too many decimal places, I have a teachable moment about following directions. Second, I can easily identify where errors have occurred and help point them out to a student. In this example, I can help the students who responded with 60.25 that they forgot to take the square root at the end. For the students whose answers start with 7.3, I can point out that they divided by 9 instead of 8. I can also tell the students who got zero for an answer that they forgot to square the deviations before adding them up. This gives them instant feedback on where to check their work. Sometimes, when the answers are up on the screen, I can see them change as students try to figure out why their answer is not the modal (most common) one. This would not be possible without being able to collect the information in real time. This is also much more effective than putting the correct answer on the board and asking the class if everyone's answer was correct. In a class of more than 100 students, some will get it right, and many will make some calculation error. Using clickers makes it easy to give everyone useful feedback rather than leaving the ones who are lost to find their own way back.

Even beyond in-class problems, clickers are extremely useful for collecting data. Answers to simple questions can assess the current climate of the class (e.g., How many students have taken a calculus class? How many have taken a previous statistics course? How many are still awake?). I can also get answers to meaningful questions (gender, handedness, race/ethnicity, etc.), but the most useful type of data we can collect goes back to being able to get students to answer data alphanumerically. This opens the door for simulating data and illustrating concepts that would be very abstract without the technology.

For example, consider a geometric random variable. We use this kind of random variable to describe situations where we are counting the number of times we try for a specific result (called a "success") which occurs with a fixed probability each time. Simple examples include counting a baseball player's number of plate appearances before he hits a home run, the number of times we have to call a household before someone answers the telephone, or the number of times we have to flip a coin before it lands heads up. We can write up a simple formula to describe this kind of random variable. Let us assume that the probability of a success is p. If X represents the number of trials until we get our success, we can define the probability for any value k (from 1 all the way up to infinity) as

$$\Pr(X = k) = (1-p)^{k-1}p$$

(If you're still reading at this point you probably feel just like my students.)

It can be pretty easy to talk about counting the number of independent Bernoulli trials until we observe a success. We can talk about the idea of a fixed probability of success and lay out a nice distribution function to show the way the probabilities are assigned to each value the random variable can take on. All the p's and X's and math will be very interesting to about 10 people in the class, and the remainder will be imagining themselves anywhere else in the world but my classroom, and with very good reason! Instead, I can ask the students to take out a quarter and participate in an experiment. Part of the fun here is teaching a classroom of 100 students the right way to flip a coin. I ask the students to flip a coin and record the number of times they had to flip it until they observe a heads. Before I had clickers, I had to ask the students how many got a heads on their first flip and count the number of hands in the air, and do that repeatedly until every student flipped a heads. Now, with clickers, I can do all kinds of neat things. I can draw three curves on the board and ask the students which one seems like it might be most appropriate for describing the shape of the data we are about to see: Will the result look symmetric or will it looked skewed to the left or right? Because we know how many students are participating, I can ask the students about how many people will say they flipped the coin and got a heads on the first try. Most of them will say half, but some could guess a totally different number (and I can watch them change as they realize where they might have gone wrong). Then I can ask them to enter their result as a number.

Many great teachable moments open up when we introduce clickers into the activity. I get a nicely drawn histogram on the board from real data we collected on the spot and a mostly clean data set of counts to work with and illustrate the concept that reaches so many more students than the formula and examples ever could. We can see the shape of the histogram and talk about why it is skewed to the right; we can talk about expected values and why our data do not quite match what we should have seen under ideal circumstances. In fact, I use this same data later on in the semester to test the goodness of the fit of the geometric model to the data we generate in class. We can look at the results of the experiment and discuss the idea of a geometric random variable in a way that talking about abstract concepts just misses. Class becomes interesting and interactive. Students are actually participating in the process of learning about something really important and useful, and the example will stick with them much longer than the formula ever will. Also, thanks to the clickers helping out with the data collection, the students do not have to wait 20 minutes for me to count and recount the number of hands in the air for each data value. This is a huge boon in a large class like mine.

I take advantage of another useful demonstration to teach the normal distribution. This is also referred to as the Gaussian distribution, but most people know it as the "bell curve." This is one of the most important probability distributions, because it applies to almost everything we can measure. It applies to not only standardized tests and growth curves, but also to heights, weights, and a host of other continuous measures we observe in populations of any kind. To show that this is true, I can ask students to enter their heights (in inches or centimeters), their weights (in pounds or kilograms), and even their body mass index (after telling them how to calculate it) into the clicker. When I put the histogram on the board, they can see the normal curve for their measures. I can even ask only the males or females to participate to show that the distribution is the same but the mean and variance may change based on gender. This is using the class's own data, not something I make up to illustrate the point. These are data actually occurring in nature. They are real data, and it is thanks to the clickers that I can show them in this way. Imagine trying to do this without a clicker in a class of 100 students. A teacher could ask each student to

1. walk up to the computer in the front of the room and enter his or her data into a spreadsheet;
2. answer a questionnaire at the beginning of the semester and hope for 100% response; or
3. ask for a show of hands for each value.

Choosing option 1 means that the whole class period will be spent having students typing into the computer and talking with their friends (probably not about statistics!) while they wait for the rest of the class. Choosing option 2 means a fraction of the class will participate, because we never get 100% response. Option 3 is a scene from a statistical horror movie, introducing imprecision and bias. With clickers, it is as simple as getting the students to type in their value. In one minute of class time, we can have 100 or more data points and a nice computer-drawn graph on the screen to illustrate the normal distribution. I can do three or four different examples in less time than it would take to collect a single data point in any of the nonclicker options.

An additional component of the clicker that I find particularly helpful is the availability of smartphone application versions of the technology. At first, this was a less-than-adequate alternative, because the alphanumeric option was unavailable. Now, students can participate in all of the in-class exercises and demonstrations using their laptop, tablet, or smartphone. Although we have not yet taken the next step of streaming the class live on the Internet, I am interested in looking into using the web-based clicker technology to allow students to participate in class even if the class is meeting virtually. This would have been invaluable last year, when blizzards closed my institution for two weeks.

When I first started working with clickers, the technology had been around for a while, but the alphanumeric clickers were still fairly new. The smartphone app option was limited to the basic clicker types, and students who wanted to use the app were unable to participate in some of the interactive components. Now, apps allow students to enter alphanumeric data as well, so students have a host of options for their clicker technology. They can buy the clicker from the bookstore, or they can download it to their phone or tablet. For many students, this is preferable to carrying yet another piece of technology around from class to class.

There are still some aspects of the clicker that limit its usefulness in the class, however. At this point, the clicker can only collect data on one item at a time. This is great for interactive opportunities in class but less helpful if I want to use clickers to collect information on an in-class assessment like a quiz or test. As of now, I administer multiple-choice/true-false exams to my students and collect their answers via Scantron. I have heard that the clicker technology is moving toward self-paced data collection. The only drawback to a change like this is not having a record of the students' responses to the exam or a way to archive and process the information to provide aggregated feedback to the students regarding their collective performance. If the technology ever reaches the utility level of the Scantron and collective information provided by the scanner, I will strongly consider replacing the scanner with the clicker for this part of class, as well.

Clickers also do not eliminate the problem of students erring with the technology. On the paper forms, they may make a transcription error and fill in the wrong bubble on their answer sheet. With clickers, they may mean to choose one option but accidentally hit another. The bigger problem here is that there will be no record of the student's answer choices for him or her to review unless the device somehow provides that information. This would require a complete redesign of the technology, which may be a long time coming.

Another possible shortcoming of the system is that, as of now, I have yet to figure out a way to store results from each question in a large spreadsheet to build a class-level data set with multiple items. Although it is very nice to demonstrate results with real data in real time in the classroom, it would be even better to be able to take different data elements and use them later on in the class to illustrate even more useful points. For example, we can look at the distribution of heights in the class when we collect the data in real time. To collect the data on gender requires a resetting of the device, and we lose the data on heights. If there were a way to save the data in a running sheet, we could use the data later to compare the mean heights across gender and see if there is actually a significant difference. We could look at t-tests, correlations, contingency tables, and a host of other analyses using the data the students provided themselves. We could even save the data from year to year and investigate trends in the classes over time. A running data session would exponentially expand the possibilities of clickers in any statistics class.

There is no doubt in my mind that technology is essential for teaching today's students. This is particularly true in service courses like mine, in which the bulk of the students are nonmajors and are typically uninterested in the material itself. Because many of them do not have an extensive background in mathematics, they find the theoretical concepts too abstract and hard to follow. For these students, it is much more valuable to teach the concepts than it is to waste their time "going under the hood" and showing them how and why the concepts work. Being able to demonstrate concepts with simulations and applets reaches a much wider audience than scrawling a host of formulas and symbols on the board. I use SAS to illustrate concepts like the central limit theorem, confidence intervals, and p-values. We can look at the effects of small sample sizes and nonnormal populations and discuss the appropriateness of the methods in a way that the theory itself would never begin to touch. Simulation is invaluable for debunking statistical myths (like $n = 30$ as the magic threshold for normality) and demonstrating a concept (like unbiased and biased estimators). Some of my students watch me write an SAS program out of the blue on the screen and seem pretty impressed that it actually works when I run it. (Honestly, sometimes I am, too.) They can watch the demonstration and see the point, but it is a very passive experience. Some of them may come away from the lesson questioning some of the things they have read or been taught prior to my class, but most of them may not think about those concepts again. Real learning happens when I can take the illustration to the next level by engaging the students and involving them in the process by using the data they have collected with their own devices. Having the students take an active role in the class gets them interested and excited about the material in ways a traditional lecture environment simply cannot. My physics professor knew he was safe from getting knocked flat; I think he also knew there were some doubters out there that would be really impressed at the end of the show. I know what the answers are going to be before I run my simulations and experiments in my class. I can tell by the oohs and aahs when I show the graph on the board that the students are just as impressed with the demonstration as I was with that pendulum all those years ago. I am convinced that the interactivity enabled by clickers can improve student learning across the health sciences, especially when quantitative reasoning can help us understand a phenomenon in an aggregate population.

7

When the Lesson Is in the Question

Illuminating Research Methodology Using Clickers

Christopher H. Wade

On the first day of my research methods course for undergraduate nurses, I ask students the following question:

Which of these choices best matches your opinion?
1. I enjoy helping patients, so I don't need a higher salary.
2. I have no opinion about my patients or salary.
3. I dislike helping patients, so I need a higher salary.

Unsurprisingly, the class fills with loud murmurs as they try to pick which unappealing option best matches their views. When the results of the poll are displayed on the screen, answer 2 typically gets the most votes. With a delighted smile and obviously feigned sincerity, I offer the class my brilliant interpretation of this data: "BSN nursing students do not have strong opinions about helping patients or their wages." Then I ask them what they think about my conclusions.

I can assure you that student response is immediate, assertive, and often amused at the sheer absurdity of the situation. Once the problematic wording has been addressed, we move on to talk about why this exercise is important. Specifically, we explore the power dynamics inherent to research, the value of piloting questions, and the responsibilities of researchers in designing their studies. By asking a poorly designed question and using the data to generate a fallacious conclusion, I was able to goad students into a critical frame of mind that subjects the research process to scrutiny, analysis, and improvement.

One of the core challenges for research methodology instructors is that students rarely arrive in the classroom with a burning desire to learn about literature review techniques, key study designs, or data analysis tools. Research courses are often seen as a hoop through which to jump, given that the topic is a requirement for graduation in a wide range of fields. As a result, an instructor has dual responsibilities: providing an introduction to a broad scope of new material while also inspiring students to care about the topic.

Nurturing a fascination with research among students is where classroom response systems (or clickers) hold the greatest potential for research methods courses. Studies have repeatedly demonstrated that clickers can increase student engagement by encouraging participation, generating discussion, and directing teaching to areas of student need (Cain & Robinson, 2008; Caldwell, 2007; De Gagne, 2011; Klein & Kientz, 2013). I believe clickers are particularly well suited for research methods courses because students need a deep understanding of questions—what makes a good question, the best ways of asking a question, and strategies for answering a question. Clickers provide a new tool for answering questions in real time, which opens a surprising number of doors for research methods pedagogy.

This chapter is devoted to exploring the ways clickers can help bring the research process to life for students. In it, I will briefly explore the available evidence on using clickers to teach research. I will then present examples of creative ways that clickers can be used to illustrate research and match those approaches with key learning goals. I will close with a detailed case study that describes how clickers can be used to facilitate a term-long, in-class research project.

CURRENT EVIDENCE ON THE USE OF CLICKERS TO TEACH RESEARCH METHODOLOGY

Recommendations for best practices in research methods pedagogy are still in their formative stages, although increasing attention is being devoted to this crucial area of instruction (Garner, Wagner, & Kawulich, 2009; Wagner, Garner, & Kawulich, 2011). Nonetheless, a common theme in the literature emphasizes that research methods courses should integrate active learning strategies that encourage students to take a role in their own learning (Wagner et al., 2011). This can occur through a range of activities, such as group discussions, case-study exercises, and in-class research projects. Aliaga and colleagues (2012) recommended that instructors use real data for learning activities focused on statistical analysis. This can contextualize the learning activity for students, and when students have a role in creating the data, they have a better understanding and recall of the lesson (Slamecka & Graf, 1978).

The use of clickers in classroom settings has been shown to have considerable potential for improving student engagement and success. This finding has been reviewed extensively elsewhere, and general recommendations for the instructional use of clickers have been developed (Beatty & Gerace, 2009; Caldwell, 2007; De Gagne, 2011; Klein & Kientz, 2013). Although clickers can be applied to recommended active learning and the collection of real data, relatively few studies have explored these potential uses in the context of research methods courses. Some initial data suggests that typical ways of implementing clickers improves learning, specifically the use of regular clicker questions to assess student knowledge and promote discussion (Khan, 2013; Kyei-Blankson, 2009). Other studies on the use of clickers to conduct in-class experiments have generally shown promising indicators of high student enthusiasm, lively discussion, and improved learning (Cleary, 2008; Haidet, Hunt, & Coverdale, 2002; McGowan & Vaughan, 2011; Micheletto, 2011). Although further research is needed, the current evidence provides reasons to be optimistic about the use of clickers to enhance research methodology courses.

STRATEGIES FOR USING CLICKERS TO ACHIEVE A RANGE OF LEARNING OBJECTIVES

Virtually all research methodology courses will have some version of the following student learning objectives in their syllabi:

- recognize key concepts in research design and implementation
- demonstrate an understanding of how to develop research questions, collect data, and interpret study findings
- exhibit the ability to critically assess the quality of published research

Clickers can support these learning goals in a number of ways, as demonstrated by the examples presented in Table 7.1.

An instructor might find it helpful to see how specific clicker exercises match up with different learning goals. To provide a theoretical framework for these pairings, I have used the revised version of Bloom's taxonomy in Table 7.1 (Anderson et al., 2001). This instructional framework describes how cognitive processes are broken down into six skills: the learner's ability to remember, understand, apply, analyze, evaluate, and create. These skills have been listed in order of increasing complexity, although this hierarchy is just a rule of thumb and exceptions exist. Many courses that use clickers focus on the remembering and understanding categories (for example, by using a

Table 7.1 Strategies for Achieving Different Learning Objectives Using Clickers

Clicker Use	Bloom's Taxonomy	Approach	Examples	Desired Outcome
Introduce New Concept	Remember Analyze Create	Instructor uses a question to introduce new idea in research without providing prior information about the topic.	• See example at beginning of the chapter. • Students read a passage from a flawed methods section of a paper. Use clickers to identify area with the problem and discuss.	• Critical thinking • Student empowerment
Check Attention and Recall	Remember Understand	Typical clicker usage. Instructor asks a question about material that has been covered.	• After teaching a lecture on data types, check whether students can correctly identify dichotomous, nominal, ordinal, interval, and ratio data. Explain correct answers.	• Immediate feedback on comprehension • Target areas needing improvement
Collect Student Opinions on Quality	Apply Analyze Evaluate	Instructor asks students to express their beliefs about quality of information.	• Students read a research article and discuss quality in groups. Use clickers to rank components of article. Launch discussion by asking why students chose certain rankings. • Students provide feedback to one another to improve research presentations.	• Critical thinking • Practice applying knowledge • Engagement and peer participation • Encourage debate
Illustrate Study Designs	Understand Apply	Instructor shows how different studies are designed using mini in-class experiments.	• Using a basic question students can easily answer (e.g., one about the relationship between exposure to sports and fan status), the instructor shows how different designs (case control, time series, RCT, etc.) could be used and collects data to demonstrate effects. See Haidet, Hunt, and Coverdale (2002) for an extended example.	• Experiential illustration of ways to gather data • Appreciation for limitations

Activity	Bloom's Level	Method	Example	Benefits
Teach Qualitative Research Skills	Understand Apply Analyze Evaluate	Instructor teaches skill and then gathers opinions on interpretation. Used to motivate discussion.	Students code selected qualitative transcripts. Designations are collected with clickers. Differences of opinion are discussed. Students watch video of interview. Share opinions of skills demonstrated and affective responses of participants. Discussion follows.	• Experiential awareness of the challenges in processing qualitative data • Skills at resolving differences of opinion
Initiate Research Ethics Debates	Apply Analyze Evaluate	Instructor presents controversial ethics case study to students. Collects opinions. Used to launch discussion.	Describe Nazi medical experiments. Ask whether potentially life-saving data that was obtained unethically should still be used later on. Students identify arguments from either perspective.	• Helps increase awareness of diversity of opinion by voicing anonymous minority views
Students Vote on Course Direction	Create	Students come up with options for research topic areas. Instructor allows students to vote on preferred topics.	Students identify and evaluate research papers on a topic currently in the news (e.g., MMR vaccines, personalized medicine, the Affordable Care Act, etc.). Students vote to select area.	• Increase student engagement by allowing their interests to drive learning
Reveal and Illustrate Researcher Biases	Analyze Evaluate	Instructor asks students questions in ways that can illustrate how biases occur in research.	To demonstrate the observer-expectancy effect, ask a question and imply that students' ability to answer will be poor. Ask another and suggest it is easy. Compare results to other cohorts where the biasing statements were reversed. See Cleary (2008) for an example.	• Critical thinking • Develop personal awareness of susceptibility to bias
Students Design and Implement Survey	Understand Apply Analyze Evaluate Create	Students select hypotheses and develop survey questions. Conduct survey and analyze results.	See extended case study in this chapter.	• Personal experience with both conducting research and being a participant • Insight into challenges and benefits of research

multiple-choice question to assess whether the students remember a specific term or concept). However, research methodology courses are well situated to use clickers for more complex cognitive tasks, as shown in Table 7.1 and discussed in the case study on in-class research that follows. Higher-level activities could, for instance, include exploring the complexities of conducting qualitative coding processes, involving students in acting out different study designs, or developing insights into research ethics debates. In fact, real-time data collection provides so many opportunities for teaching research that the ways clickers can be used is primarily limited by the creativity of the instructor.

The ability of students to understand unfamiliar and complex content is closely related to their actual desire to engage with the material. Therefore, the role of clickers in developing cognitive skills may be less important than their ability to encourage excitement and participation among students. The ways clickers accomplish this outcome can be understood using the affective domain framework from Bloom's taxonomy (Krathwohl, Bloom, & Masia, 1956). This framework considers the attitudinal aspects of learning, within which clickers are particularly relevant to developing students' capacity for receiving, responding, and valuing.

Willingness to Receive Information

I suspect that, rather than just "filling" students with knowledge about research methodology, instructors want their class to model the behavior of openly asking questions and seriously considering the responses that have been received. In fact, nurturing this attitude may be the most important factor in inspiring a student to pursue a career in research. Clickers provide the opportunity to do this in classrooms, not to mention collect data that actually provides answers. By asking students for feedback, attitudes, and opinions in a public way, instructors can use clickers to soften their image as the seat of all knowledge and instead take on the role of someone who enjoys asking questions. This, in turn, opens space for students to add their voices to these inquiries, because it is no longer assumed that a correct answer is already known. Teaching intellectual modesty and curiosity can help students to openly receive new information rather than feel like it is forced upon them.

Actively Responding to Ideas

When clickers are used in the classroom, it becomes readily apparent that students appreciate the opportunity to participate. Although research has demonstrated this preference (Caldwell, 2007), I can say from personal experience that students perk up when they feel like their contributions will be considered by their instructor and fellow students. I have observed the impact of clicker exercises in expressions of enjoyment, willingness to contribute to peer learning, and motivation to read carefully so that they can effectively participate.

Learning to Value Research

I believe clickers help students to value and identify with research practices. Beyond instilling an appreciation for asking questions, clickers help students to recognize that they have a stake in the class. This can be promoted by asking students to provide feedback or help make decisions that influence the direction of the course. Also, group clicker activities that integrate everyone's perspectives help create an ethic of building knowledge together. My sense is that, as a result, students gain a stronger appreciation for data, enjoy working collaboratively, and have greater investment in the course.

Although the components of learning described in Bloom's taxonomy are just one way to understand the educational process, I believe that clickers are particularly well suited to research methods pedagogy. Once the learning objectives an instructor seeks to achieve are identified, there are numerous opportunities to apply clickers in ways that both engage students and improve their ability to deeply understand new concepts.

CASE STUDY: CONDUCTING STUDENT-CENTERED IN-CLASS RESEARCH

In the interest of illustrating how clickers help students acquire an experiential understanding of the research process, I will discuss a term-long project (see Figure 7.1) that I use in my research methods class. It takes advantage of clickers' rapid data collection functions in order to give students the chance to view themselves as researchers, run through the challenges of various steps in the process, and experience the excitement of actually collecting and using data to answer their own questions.

To provide some background, the course has approximately 45 undergraduate nursing students. It is conceptually divided into three tracks: building foundational knowledge (readings and lecture), evidence-based practice (skills for finding and using research information), and a research experience (discussed here). The research track builds on itself throughout the entire term to create progressive insight into student-driven questions.

Figure 7.1   In-class research study design and example clicker applications.

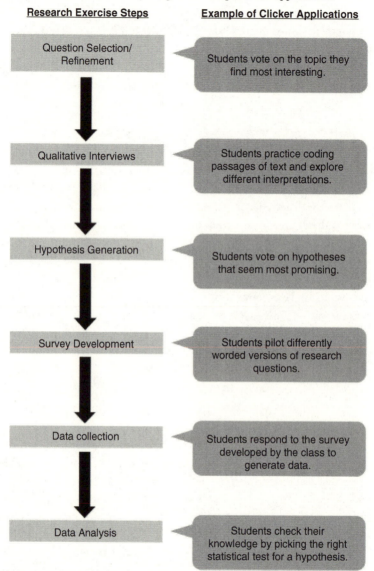

Developing the Research Question

The course research project follows a common study trajectory: conceptualization, design, data collection, and analysis. On the first day of class, I break the students up into small groups, which I challenge to identify a broad research question that (a) almost all of their fellow students would be able to provide personal answers to, and (b) they care deeply about understanding. After the class refines these questions, the students vote to obtain a favorite overarching research topic area to explore for the remainder of the term. For example, one class selected "How can UW–Bothell RN-to-BSN students manage home, work, and school life so as to reduce stress levels?"

Obviously, this overarching question needs to be narrowed, which is the topic of the next few classes. Students within each four-to-five person group proceed to develop more detailed research questions within the theme, such as "Does regular use of 15-minute breaks at work decrease stress levels?" They also split up and take turns conducting 10-minute qualitative interviews with other class members, the data from which they analyze and code to obtain themes. The insight they gain from these conversations often leads to substantial adjustments or new directions for the group and is geared toward obtaining a more specific, penetrating, and relevant question. In the last step of setup, they are asked to clearly define the relevant variables and develop a testable hypothesis.

Setting Up the Clicker Survey

Although the rapid response data obtained by clickers can be useful in the steps outlined previously (e.g., selecting a topic or coding qualitative data), they particularly shine when collecting in-class research data. This gives students a taste of the excitement that comes when one finally begins to gain insight into the answer to a novel question.

This exercise requires some preparation, with respect to both student training and materials. In class, I walk students through the range of challenges they will face in writing questions and the types of issues that can create bias (leading questions, question order, etc.). We then practice rewriting and answering questions to deal with these issues. This helps scaffold the research survey development exercise so that they feel confident designing relevant questions.

When the students are ready, I give them a set of pre-prepared survey questions, including demographic questions and a validated scale relevant to the main research outcome (in the previous example, the Perceived Stress Scale). They then develop several questions in different formats (e.g., Likert, dichotomous, and nominal/ordinal structures) that can address their research hypothesis. These questions are written down and handed in to the instructor. While the students are engaged in another activity, I quickly enter the questions into polling-ready PowerPoint slides (using integrated software from Turning Technologies, provided by my university) that enable clicker responses. This process is sped up considerably by having the demographics, scale, dichotomous, and Likert slides premade so that they only require minor modification.

Data Collection and Discussion

Conducting a student-designed survey in front of a class is the best way I have yet discovered to make data come alive. The level of engagement is obvious; it is quiet when the question is asked, but the room fills with murmurs when the answer is displayed. One of the most important lessons of this activity is the pleasure of testing our assumptions against the reality of data. In some cases, students receive confirmation that they were correct in what they initially believed, which gives them the satisfaction of being correct. In other cases, the data show a strikingly different pattern than expected, and discussion ensues. Best of all is when students honestly do not know what to expect, and they see the answer to their question materialize in front of their eyes. The real contribution of using clickers to administer these surveys is the classroom atmosphere it creates: a shared group experience of inquisitiveness and the gratification of immediate answers.

The clicker survey is an excellent launching point for class discussions that deepen student understanding. I have done this two ways: Initially, I conducted the discussion during the survey itself, making comments after each slide. This can work well for addressing immediate points. However, in more recent classes, I decided to complete the survey with only minor interruptions to point out oddities in questions or the resultant data. When complete, I launch into a more detailed discussion. This allows for more continuity and, I believe, more depth in a conversation. I start out by splitting students into their groups and asking them to share their experience of answering the survey, to identify potential flaws or areas for improvement, and to select descriptive findings that they find particularly interesting. When I bring them together for the full class conversation, students are typically eager to share their observations. We can always pull examples from the survey we just took together in order to illustrate problems with survey wording (e.g., leading, ambiguous, or double-barreled questions) and discuss strategies for collecting data with greater reliability and validity. However, this exercise goes beyond the questions themselves. Spontaneously or with little prompting, we can also explore a range of issues inherent to the study approach: sample size, investigator effects, previous knowledge biases, respondent fatigue, and so on. Although all these concepts can be addressed in a lecture, having just experienced them in the clicker survey helps students engage more deeply.

Illustrating Statistics

The most difficult section to teach in this course aims to introduce students to the basics of data analysis. This is because students typically approach statistics with a considerable amount of fear. However, I have found that by using their own data, I open up many new opportunities for engagement. Because the data they see during the clicker survey are all descriptive, I can show that the only way to reliably answer their hypotheses is to use statistical tests. In setting up for this activity, I import the data into analysis software, clean the data, and then print out relevant information (questions, demographic correlations, etc.). After working on it in groups, we then figure out together which statistical tests are needed to prove student hypotheses. Typically, the data are rich enough that I can demonstrate most major analysis techniques (e.g., chi-squared tests, ANOVA, correlations, and using regression to control for confounding variables) in answering questions about their data. I also give them the opportunity to make up new questions so I can show them the use of statistical software in real time.

Using this approach has considerable advantages. It allows me, as an instructor, to integrate a level of humor, playfulness, and theatrical inquisitiveness into our discussions. For example, different student groups hypothesized that student stress would be significantly associated with exercise, regular 15-minute breaks at work, hours spent on homework, and when homework was completed. It turns out that only one had a significant relationship, so I asked them to vote on which they thought was most promising. When they learned the answer (completing homework at the last minute was significantly associated with stress), there was a lot of nodding and comments. I cannot imagine students engaging with the data in this way if they did not take ownership of the survey questions and findings.

Considerations and Challenges

Having carried out this in-class research exercise eight times, I have encountered a number of interesting situations and challenges that are worth mentioning for those who seek to replicate the approach.

The first, and least remarkable, are technological concerns. I have had my data collection program freeze, requiring the annoyance and delay of a restart. More concerning, I once made an error saving the data, which erased them all. This forced me to repeat the survey online in order to move forward, which was mildly frustrating for the students. It is also common for students to express concerns about whether their clicker is working. I find this to be less of a concern given that they are not graded for participation, but it is still a common worry. The main lessons from these issues are (a) check your setup before using it, (b) practice using the software, and (c) cross your fingers and hope it all works. It is worth noting that both the technology and software are improving, making such errors less likely.

One should also consider the characteristics of the class. When a class is small (fewer than 20 or so), one's ability to detect significant differences and interesting descriptive patterns decreases. Of course, you will occasionally see something pop up when there is a large effect size, but there is a fairly high probability that none of your student groups will see a significant relationship when testing their hypotheses. Conversely, when a class is really large, you also could run into problems. Specifically, the survey itself can get so long in order to test all student questions that you start getting respondent fatigue. This turns a fun exercise into a burdensome chore, despite the fact that clickers are being used. This can be mitigated, however, by picking only a selection of the student questions, perhaps by putting the hypotheses up for a popularity vote or perhaps simply choosing the ones you see as most interesting.

Another caution is that the overarching desire to make this a student-directed exercise should not stop you from meddling when needed. It is very important to make sure that the questions being addressed are correctly con-structed, interesting, and unique. I have found that a sizable minority of student groups, when left alone, will gravitate toward the most obvious questions. My worst example of this was when three out of eight groups independently decided to look at the impact of exercise on stress. I did not have the time to help them refine their questions before the survey, so we ended up asking a lot of nearly identical, bland questions about frequency of exercise. This, to some extent, both decreased excitement and increased respondent fatigue. I have learned that pushing them early on to stretch their understanding by asking insightful, care-fully worded questions both improves engagement and makes them proud of their work.

I would also like to point out some situations I have encountered that are worth considering prior to doing this exercise. It is generally seen as ethical to conduct in-class research, often without formal consent, because students benefit greatly from the experience. Additionally, clickers are perfect for this purpose, because they can allow student respondents to remain anonymous. However, it is very important to remain cognizant of how small groups of students can still be singled out during data analysis. For example, I did the in-class research exercise jointly with two different sections of the same class. The first class comprised all women (not entirely uncommon in nurs-ing), and the second included a handful of men. Ultimately, the sample had a gender ratio of 9 men to 56 women. When exploring the data with the first class (all women), it was discovered that the male students had significantly higher salaries and almost all held management positions, which was a rarity among female students. The class exploded with annoyance, and more than a few expletives were directed toward male nurses. Although this is an important illustration of gender disparities, I felt compelled to remove the gender data for the second class, which included the 9 male students. This is because the male students had taken the survey with the assumption of anonymity, yet they were a small enough group that their individual income and leadership status could easily be inferred by the other students (and they likely would have experienced similar vocal displeasure from their female classmates). This issue of compromised anonymity is something to watch for in any class where a small group of students could be readily identified.

A second situation which I had not anticipated related to the content of the questions a student group put together. In this case, a group hypothesized that working the night shift would decrease the quality of nurses' sex lives. This is an entirely legitimate and interesting question. However, I had some concern around asking the class to answer questions about the frequency and quality of their sex lives, even though it was anonymous. My solution was to re-emphasize prior to the questions that anyone who was uncomfortable was welcome to not respond. Although the number of responses was slightly lower, these turned out to be far and away the most popular questions on the survey; it took a minute or two to get the class back on track afterward because they were so interested in the results. Although this example turned out fine, one could easily imagine a scenario in which offensive, discriminatory, or inflammatory questions were asked. This reiterates the importance of playing a role in refining student questions and ensuring that you have enough time to screen the questions adequately before conducting the clicker survey.

CONCLUSION

Like anyone teaching research methodology, I am deeply aware of the power this topic has to influence how students use and critique information in the world around them. As important as a thorough understanding of research is to many careers, I am just as committed to helping nurture students' ability to make evidence-based judgments when engaging with scientific and political debates. If I can also inspire at least a few students to consider embarking on a path toward pursuing their own research, I would be delighted. All of these goals require igniting a spark of interest in students, and this is where I believe clickers have tremendous potential as a tool for instructors.

The ability to quickly generate questions, rapidly collect data, and instantly visualize the results makes clickers ideal for connecting students with the research process. There are virtually unlimited ways that instructors can creatively use clickers to illuminate research; the approaches suggested previously and the case study only scratch the surface. For example, one could imagine class designs in which publishable research is conducted (Micheletto, 2011), elaborate case studies are explored (Haidet et al., 2002), or clicker-based educational games are developed (Boyle et al., 2014). Ultimately, by allowing students to create, test, and use data, clickers help inspire a level of appreciation for research that is only found in personal experience.

REFERENCES

Aliaga, M., Cobb, G., Cuff, C., Garfield, J., Gould, R., Lock, R., . . . Witmer, J. (2012). *Guidelines for assessment and instruction in statistics education: College report.* Alexandria, VA: American Statistical Association.

Anderson, L. W., Krathwohl, D. R., Airasian, P. W., Cruikshank, K. A., Mayer, R. E., Pintrich, P. R., . . . Wittrock, M. C. (2001). *A taxonomy for learning, teaching, and assessing: A revision of Bloom's taxonomy of educational objectives.* New York, NY: Longman.

Beatty, I., & Gerace, W. (2009). Technology-enhanced formative assessment: A research-based pedagogy for teaching science with classroom response technology. *Journal of Science Education and Technology, 18*(2), 146–162.

Boyle, E., MacArthur, E., Connolly, T., Hainey, T., Manea, M., Karki, A., & Van Rosmalen, P. (2014). A narrative review of games, animations and simulations to teach research methods and statistics. *Computers & Education, 74,* 1–14.

Cain, J., & Robinson, E. (2008). A primer on audience response systems: Current applications and future considerations. [Review]. *American Journal of Pharmaceutical Education, 72*(4), 1–6.

Caldwell, J. E. (2007). Clickers in the large classroom: Current research and best-practice tips. [Research Support, Non-U.S. Gov't Review]. *CBE Life Sciences Education, 6*(1), 9–20. doi: 10.1187/cbe.06-12-0205

Cleary, A. M. (2008). Using wireless response systems to replicate behavioral research findings in the classroom. *Teaching of Psychology, 35*(1), 42–44. doi: 10.1080/00986280701826642

De Gagne, J. C. (2011). The impact of clickers in nursing education: A review of literature. [Review]. *Nurse Education Today, 31*(8), e34–40. doi: 10.1016/j.nedt.2010.12.007

Garner, M., Wagner, C., & Kawulich, B. (2009). *Teaching research methods in the social sciences.* Burlington, VT: Ashgate.

Haidet, P., Hunt, D., & Coverdale, J. (2002). Learning by doing: Teaching critical appraisal of randomized trials by performing an in-class randomized trial. *Academic Medicine, 77*(11), 1161.

Khan, R. (2013, November). *Teaching first-year business statistics three ways.* Paper presented at the Lighthouse Delta 2013, Kiama, Australia.

Klein, K., & Kientz, M. (2013). A model for successful use of student response systems. *Nursing Education Perspectives, 34*(5), 334–338.

Krathwohl, D., Bloom, B., & Masia, B. (1956). *Taxonomy of educational objectives. Handbook II: Affective Domain.* New York, NY: David McKay.

Kyei-Blankson, L. (2009). Enhancing student learning in a graduate research and statistics course with clickers. *Educause Review, 32*(4). Retrieved May 27, 2015, from http://www.educause.edu/ero/article/enhancing-student-learning-graduate-research-and-statistics-course-clickers

McGowan, H., & Vaughan, J. (2011). Testing a student generated hypothesis using student data. *Teaching Statistics, 34*(2), 61–64.

Micheletto, M. (2011). Conducting a classroom mini-experiment using an audience response system: Demonstrating the isolation effect. *Journal of College Teaching & Learning, 8*(8), 1–14.

Slamecka, N. J., & Graf, P. (1978). Generation Effect—Delineation of a Phenomenon. *Journal of Experimental Psychology-Human Learning and Memory, 4*(6), 592–604. doi: 10.1037//0278-7393.4.6.592

Wagner, C., Garner, M., & Kawulich, B. (2011). The state of the art of teaching research methods in the social sciences: Towards a pedagogical culture. *Studies in Higher Education, 36*(1), 75–88. doi: 10.1080/03075070903452594

8

Using Clickers in Hospitality and Other Professional Programs

Alison J. Green

There is nothing better for a teacher than hearing students actually making up their minds when being asked for their opinion, and then making a statement. That is what my experience with using clickers in a hospitality classroom is like, and for those who are in tune with students that enjoy active, hands-on engagement in the classroom, it is fun to see the enthusiasm for learning occur right before one's eyes. When using clickers, there is a particular, satisfying sound that lets me know the students have answered a polling question, which is unique to any educational technology I have used: It is the physical act of clicking in an answer and then setting the clicker back on the desk to indicate "I have answered!" When students engage with the material using clickers, they feel that they have been counted—that their opinion matters. Primarily for that reason, I use clickers in each class that I teach, from 12 to 60 students, as part of the overall design to incorporate active learning.

As a professor teaching in a hotel college, with average class sizes of 60, and growing, I embrace anything I can use to help the students be more fully engaged, better understand the material, and be excited about learning. I also research educational technology in the hospitality classroom across the globe, and I have tried many different tools, including online, cloud-based, lecture software. After trying many new technologies, I always come back to using those little, remote transmitters, or what we call clickers.

HOSPITALITY STUDENTS

Hospitality students are a bit different from students in more traditional disciplines. Part of what we teach our students is how to serve others, how to make a great meal, how to provide outstanding customer service, or even how to problem-shoot an HVAC unit. Our classes also tend to be large. We commonly have a minimum of 60 seats and sometimes upward of 300 in a lecture hall. We also draw a disproportionate number of international students. For instance, in the introductory classes that I teach, about half of the students come from abroad. Many of the students are not yet comfortable with the English language and may find speaking in class and answering questions daunting, or they may fear getting the answer wrong. (Interestingly, we have a hotel college campus in Singapore, and we have found that most students there share a cultural upbringing in which students hold the professor in higher regard than is typical in the United States, and that teacher-centered lectures are the norm.)

As I tell my students, in the hospitality industry, we are not out to cure cancer; rather, we are out to produce the best customer service experience for our guests. When the industry is looked at this way, one can see why active learning in hospitality and other professional disciplines is so important: We must model the practice of placing the experience of those we serve above our own needs. Clickers can provide one tactic in an overall strategy of learner-centered pedagogy in professional fields.

TECHNOLOGY

Technology helps connect the students to the material, but I believe the real benefit comes from careful consideration of course design and implementation and the resultant focus on active learning. Technology such as clickers, however, provides inspiration and opportunities that an instructor can leverage to achieve that mindful course design in ways that were far less attainable a couple of decades ago. Clickers, in my experience, provide ways to turn a one-directional lecture into a set of polling questions through which we can check for understanding or lead students to revelations rather than simply handing knowledge to them. Thus, clickers, in my classes, are integral to deep learning.

Who, though, teaches the teachers how to use the devices? Although some institutions have professional consultants in information technologies, I think the best way to gain command of using clickers in class is to use clickers in class. That sounds a bit funny, but instructors must allow themselves enough time to get comfortable with the hardware and software. Give yourself time to try it out for an academic term, incorporating it in several lectures or class sessions you design. Do not give up just because something does not work the first time you try it. As with any technology, one must expect the unexpected and have a "plan B" in reserve.

The actual setup is very easy, especially if you communicate with the technology office on campus. To begin a clicker program using the technology that we have at my university (primarily i>clickers, although no one system is officially supported), all one needs is a teacher clicker, a base, and a USB port to hold the receiver, which looks like a flash drive, and each student needs a hand-held clicker (which is a radio-frequency transmitter). Because several of my colleagues use clickers in the classroom, the Office of Information Technology has installed bases in our classrooms so that when we arrive, we just have to set up our USB receivers and get ready for polling. Very little time or effort is expended when I arrive for class. All I have to do is bring a USB receiver to class, plug it into the PC, select the class, and off I go!

I have found that most students expect the instructor to be the go-to person in regard to troubleshooting the technology. For that reason, I spend a good part of a lecture during the first week reviewing how the clicker works, my classroom expectations, and how I plan to use clickers in the course. That way, if students have issues down the road, they most likely can turn to their neighbor and get some advice.

CLOUD-BASED SYSTEMS VIA STUDENTS' OWN DEVICES OR PROPRIETARY, HANDHELD DEVICES?

I have embraced both of these approaches over the years, and for me, keeping a clicker as a separate device is key. The reason for this is not what most instructors fear (students surfing the Internet); rather, it is so that the hardware is consistent with what is (unofficially) supported by the university. If there are issues with the hardware, I have the ability to troubleshoot on the spot, or I can ask a representative from the technology office to come to solve the issue with the device, computer, or classroom.

Most students today have a strong command of personal mobile devices such as tablets and smartphones. It makes sense to capitalize on their comfort with and affinity for such technologies. I personally do not fear loss of control of what happens in the classroom, but I do sometimes find that the mobile device itself tends to slow down the polling process in a classroom. When I have used software based on a smartphone or tablet application rather than a dedicated, handheld device, it seemed as if we had to wait longer for the responses to come into synchronization with the other devices in class. For that reason, I use the separate devices—the i>clicker transmitters—so that responses are displayed more rapidly (and so students are not distracted by other temptations on their devices or those of their classmates).

STUDENT ENGAGEMENT

Most instructors fundamentally understand that, across all disciplines, student engagement leads to deeper learning and to greater student satisfaction. Simply stated, participation leads to better learning outcomes. On a deeper level, students taking hold of their own learning and discovery typically stimulates a positive attitude toward the subject matter. Engagement includes three dimensions: behavioral, emotional, and cognitive (Bloom & Krathwohl, 1956).

Behavioral engagement is the way in which a student interacts with the course, for example by attending and participating in class sessions. Integrating clickers into the classroom can contribute significantly to students' behavioral engagement with a course. At its most fundamental level, taking attendance via clickers, such as by asking a question in class and identifying who has responded (most clicker technologies permit both individually identified and anonymous responses), rewards and thereby encourages attendance. Moreover, clickers promote student participation throughout a class session.

Emotional engagement entails the degree to which students enjoy class time. When using clickers, students feel more connected to the teacher and their classmates, increasing a sense of belonging. When students feel that their participation makes a difference, they in turn tend to care more about the class.

The final dimension in trying to achieve student engagement is cognitive engagement, which entails students taking responsibility for their own learning, shown, for example, when they care about getting the correct answer to a polling question and strive to learn the concepts and ideas that will lead to a correct response. Inherently, students want to answer correctly.

One can see, then, that clickers can enhance all three dimensions of student engagement, thereby increasing students' learning and pleasure.

ANONYMITY AND INTROVERTS

The field of hospitality tends to attract extroverts. The hospitality industry recruits people who are outgoing, welcoming, and good at connecting with others, because it is a people-oriented business in which employees directly and personally serve guests. This is the norm in the industry for which we are preparing our students. Nevertheless, we do have students who consider themselves introverted. We certainly want to provide active engagement opportunities for our diverse student body. Clickers offer a way for more reticent students to have voice in class. Because the aggregated data collected and immediately available in the polling slides do not have names attached, clicker technology provides a safe way for those who usually do not speak up in class to have a say.

Moreover, like many career-oriented professional degree programs, hospitality courses enroll many students for whom English is not their first language. For students less confident in English, clickers allow participation without the fear of errors in spoken English. With clickers, all students can participate equally. Especially in a course with a disproportionate number of extroverts, we can mitigate what otherwise might be conversations dominated by the more outgoing students.

USING CLICKERS FOR ACTIVE LEARNING

As a teacher in hospitality education, I know that most people do not sit and listen for more than an hour and thus are not able to absorb all of what is being taught. In fact, especially for customer-focused, professional careers like hospitality, in which people are typically on their feet for most of the day, sitting is itself a challenge. Because they are in Las Vegas, the mecca of hospitality, the majority of the students in my classes are already working part- or full-time or are undertaking internships. They are used to moving and talking at work. I keep this in mind when I design my lectures. First and foremost, I go back to Dale's (1969) cone of learning, which separates pedagogical orientations into passive and active learning. Passive learning entails reading, listening, seeing, and hearing, whereas active learning emphasizes speaking, saying, and doing. Students in hospitality and other similar professional programs respond particularly well to active learning.

Active learning makes sense for students who like to be involved, and it will lead to student participation and ultimately student engagement. This approach builds upon the students' previous knowledge and experience; the instructor presents new material in a way that enables students to apply it to their own framework. Active learning that honors students' professional experience increases the chances that students will remember the concepts for a longer period of time.

Active learning exemplifies a social constructivist (Vygotsky, 1978) pedagogical approach, for which clickers can be instrumental. The thoughtful use of clickers encourages social learning, hands-on learning, and peer-to-peer learning, which are effective in all disciplines but especially appropriate in hospitality courses, which are by nature focused on personal interactions.

DESIGNING THE LECTURE

In designing a class session that incorporates clickers and active learning, I operate from a stance in which I am the facilitator rather than the sole source of learning. To do so, I employ several kinds of clicker prompts.

I always start the class with a forced question to check for understanding of a previous lecture. This answer is either "yes" or "no," "agree" or "disagree," or "a" or "b," and it takes very little time for the student to read the question and respond. Once the responses are collected, I share the bar chart that is automatically constructed by the i>clicker software based upon the responses, and then I take time to review key concepts if needed. Forcing students into one response or the other often stimulates further discussion, which reinforces the previous class's main lesson.

The second type of clicker question aims to aid higher-order thinking. Such a question may lead off with "If you could . . ." or "What would you do if . . ." and then offers up to five potential responses, labeled "a" through "e." If roughly 75% or more of the students get the answer correct, I move on. If fewer than 75% understand the answer, I take the opportunity to have the students chat with their neighbor and then come up with what they think is the correct answer. I then poll the class again, and I either move on or, if under 75% answered correctly, I offer a mini-lecture.

Mini-lectures can be prepared in advance and are ready to go when the results of a clicker poll suggest that one would be helpful, but I am more likely to use storytelling to link the topic to the real-world hotel or hospitality setting. The mini-lecture could therefore entail teaching on the fly, drawing upon the instructor's professional expertise. Students in professional fields such as hospitality seem especially to enjoy real-life stories. Because so many of the students are currently working in the industry, the impromptu mini-lecture also offers a chance for students to contribute their own experiences to the discussion.

In addition to using clickers in a thoughtfully designed lecture, I also enjoy polling on the fly. For instance, if I want to know how many people in the room understood instructions that I have just verbally presented, I ask that they click in with their answer. I thereby immediately get the pulse of the classroom and can determine whether the majority of students understand the instructions. If the answer is "yes," I keep going; if the answer is "no," I take a few minutes to clarify the instructions or have students explain the assignment to their confused peers.

ASSESSMENT

Looking for new ways to figure out if what I am discussing in class is making sense to the learners, I like to assess the learning outcomes. This happens both formally and informally, following summative and formative assessment activities. The summative assessments are in the form of short quizzes in class, capturing the responses, assigning points to each question, and then uploading the final scores via the learning management system. I usually ask five to ten questions, some at the more foundational levels of learning (e.g., what Bloom's taxonomy refers to as "remembering" or "understanding") and some at the more sophisticated levels (e.g., "applying" or "evaluating").

Formative assessment entails a series of questions on topics that have been covered in prior lectures. After class, I review the responses, looking for trends in comprehension and application to real-world situations, and then loop back in the next class meeting and review what, if anything, needed clarification.

I have found that both summative and formative assessment, using clickers, is a good alternative to tests, essays, and traditional paper-based or Scantron quizzes. My students report that informal clicker assessment reduces their test anxiety. When used throughout the semester, formative assessment via clickers helps me adjust to student misunderstanding or confusion before it is too late, because I would otherwise discover such problems only after administering the final exam.

CLICKERS: THE GOOD

Using clickers in the hospitality classroom helps to get students engaged with the subject matter and with their fellow students, and it enables me to employ both planned and impromptu lessons. Moreover, because students in professional programs such as hospitality often have significant work experience, clickers help me capitalize on their knowledge. For example, I can ask students to give their opinions, via clickers, about developments and news in the hospitality industry or trends they see in Las Vegas hotels. The results of these on-the-fly polls connect theory with their own practice and often generate lively—even heated—discussions.

CLICKERS: THE BAD

Technology sometimes fails. Just this semester, the software crashed during a polling session, requiring a time-wasting reboot, frustrating both the students and me. The i>clicker technology we use at the University of Nevada, Las Vegas, also presents challenges associated with moving from my office Macintosh computer to the PC in my classroom. Even after years of using clickers, I sometimes struggle with cross-platform transitions.

CLICKERS: THE UGLY

I would be remiss if I did not share my stories of students cheating by using clickers. As sad as I was to find out that students cheat with clickers by having a friend "click in" on their behalf, I will not stop using the devices; I believe that if students want to cheat, they will, and more importantly—especially in the field of hospitality in which lack of knowledge and skills can result in embarrassment or even discipline—cheating carries its own consequences. This has happened on several occasions, and I still spot-check to make sure that the number of responses represents how many students are in class. I do so by having the students click in on a polling slide and, once the numbers are locked in, put their name on a piece of paper (along with their response to another question that they have to write down) and submit it. Finally, before I wrap up the class period, I ask that they count off, so that I have a final number to compare against the responses and then against the written names. I usually do this once in the span of the 16-week semester.

THE FUTURE

As I write this piece about clickers, I ponder what will happen in the future in regard to technology in the classroom. Some unimagined technology will undoubtedly take the place of clickers. What is unlikely to change, however, is the desire of instructors to keep current with their students, to help them connect the dots between theory and practice, and to enable them to apply what they learn to the industry in which they pursue their careers. In the hospitality industry, we think that the most essential traits of a practicing professional are communication skills, emotional intelligence, and the ability to relate to others in a service environment. From my present knowledge and understanding, I know that clickers are an efficient, low-cost way to help students engage with the material, their peers, and me, and to walk away from a lecture—and their education as a whole—engaged and motivated. I am eager to discover what tools the future might contribute to this pursuit, but for now I will continue to use clickers in my classroom.

REFERENCES

Bloom, B. S., & Krathwohl, D. R. (1956). *Taxonomy of educational objectives: The classification of educational goals, by a committee of college and university examiners. Handbook I: Cognitive domain.* New York, NY: Longmans.

Dale, E. (1969). *Audio-visual methods in teaching* (3rd ed.). New York, NY: Holt, Rinehart & Winston.

Vygotsky, L. S. (1978). *Mind and society.* Cambridge, MA: Harvard University Press.

9

Using Clickers to Train Tutors in College Learning Centers

Ashley Harris Paul

I t's training day. I stand at the front of a large classroom, along with the other Tallahassee Community College (TCC) Learning Commons learning specialists, staring into the faces of almost 100 peer and professional tutors. Behind me is a Smart Board projecting the slide shown in Figure 9.1.

I restate the question on the slide: "Police, or no police?"

The tutors hold up their clickers and frantically chime in as if they are on *Jeopardy!*, and this answer determines whether or not they make it to the final round. Once all 96 tutors have submitted their answers, a colleague hits the enter button, revealing a bar graph on the screen showing that 47% said to call the police and 53% said not to get the police involved. We then have the basis for an animated discussion.

The tutors in the Learning Commons at TCC deal with more than 11,000 unique students per semester; in order to ensure that our services are comprehensible and consistent, we train our tutors using a program that is nationally accredited by the College Reading and Learning Association (CRLA). This program requires tutors to complete a certain number of face-to-face training hours covering topics such as study skills, learning styles, and other more sensitive topics like handling difficult students. For these trainings, we often deal with large groups, so we have to come up with innovative methods of teaching these topics—most of which are nuanced, without easy right-or-wrong answers—to tutors. One way we do this is through the use of clickers in training sessions.

Derek Bruff (2009) has shown that the "use of clickers often increases student attendance, participation, and enjoyment of class" (p. 5). Clickers can have similar effects on employee training, and we have discovered their benefits by using them to train our tutors. Using clickers helps keep tutors engaged

Figure 9.1   Scenario 1.

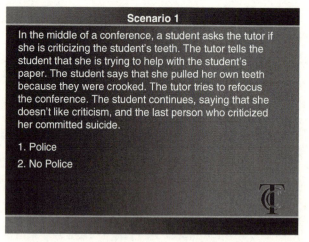

in the subject matter, helps deal with time constraints, encourages more reticent tutors to participate, and appeals to a variety of learners.

For a couple of years, we were using the same lessons and teaching methods, and we found that when tutors were actually faced with situations in which the training should have helped them, they were not utilizing the skills because they had not retained the information learned in training. We suspected this was due to lack of engagement with the material, so last year, we wrote a mini-grant to purchase two clicker systems—enough to use when training all of the tutors at once. The grant was approved, and we finally had the clickers, so the next step became how to use them most effectively. Because of the variety of topics covered in training, we had to determine which topics would be best suited for this type of interaction. The "Handling Difficult Students" lesson immediately came to mind, because we used to play a game called "Police, No Police," in which we would offer the tutors a scenario, and they would hold up either a sign with "Police" on it or one with "No Police" on it. However, we noticed during this game that some people would not hold the sign up at all and others would wait until everyone else had chosen, look around, and then make a decision, so instead of actually considering the scenario and how they might react in it, they were just copying others' answers. Thus, they were not always actively engaged in the material. They could easily zone out or skip the question. Furthermore, there was no clear way to determine what the exact percentages were, because we had insufficient time either to count the nearly 100 signs being held in the air or to speak with every tutor to ensure that he or she understood the information.

Finally, we wanted to make sure that no matter how we revised the lesson, it still appealed to multiple learning styles, which is important to ensure the retention of the information. That is when we transformed the "Police, No Police" activity into a lesson that incorporated clickers. We created a PowerPoint presentation that presented a number of scenarios to the tutors in which they had to decide whether or not to call the police. A poll was incorporated into the lesson so that tutors could weigh in, and their answers were displayed in bar graph format. This lesson was important because we had faced the problem of tutors calling the police for every little thing that went wrong when many of these issues could have been handled in-house, and because handling difficult students was one of the training topics required to become a CRLA-certified tutor.

ACTIVE ENGAGEMENT

One of the issues we often have with training sessions is that tutors find them boring and immediately disengage from the content, especially in a large-group setting. Consequently, we started using clickers. We first used the newly formatted "Police, No Police" game in the preservice training of spring 2012, which was also the first time we used clickers. As we passed the clickers out, the tutors immediately took an interest. They examined them closely and pushed a few buttons. "What are these?" they asked. We told them about the clickers and explained how the game worked. The tutors perked up and focused on the screen. Even some people who were sitting toward the back moved forward so that they could see better. We presented the scenarios, one of which is shown in Figure 9.2.

Figure 9.2   Scenario 2.

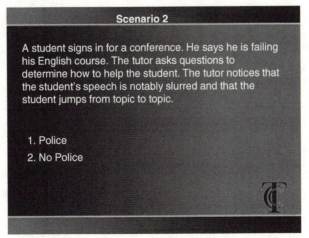

We had the students think about it and then enter their answer. The results showed that 33% said we should get the police involved, and 67% said we should not. Now that we had presented the material to them, we wanted to further engage them by discussing this situation and thinking critically about how to handle it. (This was an actual incident that occurred in the Learning Commons.) Using the "think-vote-share" method from the book *Teaching with Classroom Response Systems* (Bruff, 2009), we had the tutors pair off and discuss the situation and why they thought that they should or should not get the police involved. This method is also known as peer instruction (PI), which was made popular by Eric Mazur, a physics professor at Harvard University. PI involves the tutors talking with one another to "share and discuss their answers" (Bruff, 2009, p. 14). As Bruff noted, "Asking students to discuss a given question with their peers is a way of actively engaging them in course material" (p. 16). Just as instructors engage students in the classroom through this approach, we engaged tutors during training sessions. As we walked around the room listening to the conversations, we were delighted to hear the tutors working through the situation and talking about whether or not it called for police involvement. This got the tutors to not only think about the information, but also to engage with their colleagues, a valuable method for creating team camaraderie. Our building is separated into two floors—math and science downstairs and communications upstairs—so some of the tutors had never even met one another. Creating more opportunities in the training for tutors to interact not only with us and the material, but also with each other, is a great way to foster relationships among the tutors. As Bruff (2009) noted, "Students [and tutors] often appreciate the chance to hear from and get to know each other." Such interaction is especially important among colleagues because it creates a cohesive work environment.

After the discussion, we asked the tutors to vote again. This time, 100% of them said that the police should not be involved, which indeed was the correct response. This led to a large group discussion about what the plan of action should be if this scenario occurred. At this point, we were not simply presenting boring information through a PowerPoint presentation; we had gotten the tutors personally involved by using clickers. Kumar Laxman (2011) found that "clickers increased opportunities for faculty-student and student-student interactions, particularly during lecture times which have traditionally been passive learning experiences" (p. 1298). Our training sessions had become passive learning experiences, but by incorporating clickers, we offered a new way of introducing this material to the tutors so that they became actively engaged with it. They were engaging with not only the information, but also one another, which was beneficial to their retention of best practices in their work.

TIME CONSTRAINTS

In a large-group setting such as that of our training sessions, we are faced with time constraints and may not be able to talk to everyone. According to Bruff (2009), "Some students are not able to volunteer answers during class simply due to time constraints" (p. 198). We find this to be true of our training sessions. Because we have only an hour to deliver a lesson, it is often difficult to determine whether all participants comprehend the information. By using clickers, we can rest assured that all tutors are in fact weighing in because we know the number of people in attendance, and with each question, we see a tally of all the votes that have been cast. (Each person can vote only once.) As Bruff (2009) noted, "One reason to use classroom response systems is that they have the ability to allow every student to respond to a question and the ability to display the distribution of student response for all students to see" (p. 6). Using clickers "gives every student [or tutor] in the class [or training] the opportunity to respond . . . without having to wait to be called on, thus increasing the number of opportunities to respond for all students in the class" (Blood & Gulchak, 2013, p. 248). Thus, the use of clickers helps us ensure that everyone has the time and motivation to answer.

In addition to using clickers in a teaching game, we also use them to review information for tutors. In another lesson, "Review of Referral Skills," we use a multiple-choice "quiz" to review materials that we have already gone over and to ascertain tutor retention. One of the primary tasks of a Learning Commons tutor is to be able to point students in the right direction. Because the Learning Commons is a hub for TCC students, it is often the place students come when they need help with something—academic or otherwise. For example, students may come to the Learning Commons to ask about registration or financial aid. The tutors therefore must know where to send students to obtain the information they seek. To help the tutors know where to refer students, we provide a CRLA-required topic lesson called "Referral Skills." During this lesson, we go over the most common questions students ask and the services students most often ask about. At the beginning of each semester, during "Boot Camp," a shorter training day to refresh tutors on policies and procedures, we highlight and review important past CRLA topics. One of these reviews is based on the "Referral Skills" lesson. See Figures 9.3 and 9.4 for examples.

Figure 9.3   Where does a student go for advising?

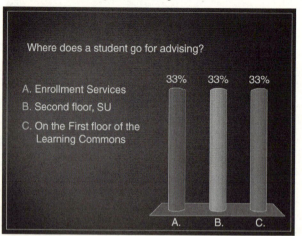

Figure 9.4   How does a student check out a study room at the library?

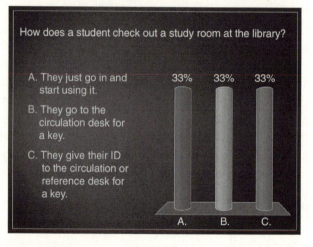

If we were conducting this quiz in a traditional, paper format, we would not be able to immediately determine the answers and therefore would not have time to discuss the correct answers within the training session. We would have to collect the quizzes, grade them, and go over the answers at a later date. By using clickers, we can determine immediately what the tutors know and address issues accordingly. This format tests the tutors in a timely fashion to see that the tutors know where to send students. As Blood and Gulchak (2013) pointed out, "Student response systems allow teachers [trainers] to receive immediate feedback about student understanding of information" (p. 247). If everyone gets the correct answer, we know that all of the tutors will refer students to the correct location. If some people choose the incorrect answer, we have the opportunity to identify the correct answer and explain why it represents a better response. This "in-the-moment" method allows us to use our time wisely, because we can determine what information to focus on and what information the tutors already understand. In the aforementioned quiz, we ask the other tutors to elaborate on the answer when some tutors answer incorrectly. For example, when we ask the tutors how to check out a study room, and someone says that students do not have to check them out, then we might ask another tutor to respond to this. That way, the tutors hear from one another and not just from the leaders. Thus, using clickers for this lesson review allows us to determine the knowledge and retention of the tutors within the allotted time period.

GIVING EVERYONE A VOICE

Clickers give reticent tutors the courage to speak up even if they are only doing so through the click of the button, and they ensure that everyone participates. Bruff maintained that "without clickers, often the vocal minority of students . . . ends up making the decisions," but, with clickers, "more student voices are heard, and the majority makes the decision instead" (Bruff, 2009, p. 8). This is also true when dealing with tutors during training sessions. The outspoken few tend to take over the discussion, making it difficult for shyer people to contribute. For example, when we originally did the "Police, No Police" lesson with the paper signs, certain tutors who had a strong opinion and who were not afraid to voice it took over the conversation. We have tutors from all over the world, and some have cultural backgrounds that make it difficult for them to voice opinions openly. By using clickers, we found that tutors who typically did not speak during training sessions began to chime in and make their opinions heard, especially after they had the chance to think about the scenario fully and discuss it in small groups. And even if they did not actually speak, their vote counted because they used the clicker to input their answer. Thus, by using clickers, we increased tutor participation, which in turn ensured an increase in retention of the material.

In addition, some people might avoid answering at all, because "sometimes students may feel reluctant to volunteer an idea or thought because they are unsure where others . . . stand" (Blood & Gulchak, 2013, p. 251). Some tutors might not want to answer because they do not want to look silly in front of their peers. And when there is a large of group of people, it is difficult for us to ensure that they are all answering. A student who does not want to be involved can easily hide in the sea of paper signs being held in the air, and we could not necessarily tell if someone was not answering. With clickers, we can guarantee participation because we do not move on until all participants have registered their answer. As Blood and Gulchak (2013) noted, "This forced participation gives each student time to think about the question and make a decision" (p. 249). Thus, using clickers helps ensure that everyone is participating and having his or her voice heard.

CONCLUSION

Overall, using clickers as a training tool in our learning center has proved very beneficial in engaging the tutors and helping them retain the information. We have seen a dramatic increase in tutors handling difficult situations on their own since presenting the "Police, No Police" lesson in this new format. Furthermore, tutors were actively engaged in the lesson during the training session, and every tutor was given a voice. Just as in the classroom, clickers can be incorporated effectively into employee training activities to make them more enjoyable, because most people "appreciate the interactivity that a response system adds" (Bruff, 2009, p. 130). We give the tutors surveys to fill out after the session, and we have found that the lessons that incorporate the use of clickers have scored favorably among the tutors. As Bruff (2009) found, "Use of clickers often increases student attendance, participation, and enjoyment of classes" (p. 5). It seems to have done the same for training sessions—making them more fun for tutors and more effective for improving the quality of their work.

REFERENCES

Blood, E., & Gulchak, D. (2013). Embedding "clickers" into classroom instruction: Benefits and strategies. *Intervention in School and Clinic, 48,* 246–253.

Bruff, D. (2009). *Teaching with classroom response systems: Creating active learning environments.* San Francisco, CA: Jossey-Bass.

Laxman, K. (2011). A study on the adoption of clickers in higher education. [Special issue]. *Australasian Journal of Educational Technology, 27*(8), 1291–1303. Retrieved December 15, 2014, from http://www.ascilite.org.au/ajet/ajet27/laxman.html

10

The Answer Is at Hand

Cell Phones as Transitional Educational Technology

Alyson Indrunas

Please take the role of being a student seriously; be on time to class and *always turn off your cell phone while you are in my class.*

—my syllabus circa 2007

Around the time I started teaching, in 2001, cell phones were growing in popularity but were not yet the ubiquitous part of everyday life that they are today. As a teacher, I took pride in the sarcastic shaming of my students as they tried to send text messages during my class. Italics in my syllabus established an edict to banish all cell phone use. My colleagues, however, quickly outpaced me with their contempt for this new technology. In discussions about classroom management, I always upheld the belief that students could do whatever they wanted in my class as long as they did not interfere with the learning of others. As long as they were done quietly, I often ignored sleeping, doing work for other courses, and various other indicators of uncommitted student behavior. Texting, however, would always get my attention.

Hearing the disapproval in the voices of my colleagues as they talked about their students and their cell phones made me reflect on my own youth. I spent my entire high school career writing notes to my friends—a skill, it turns out, that has served me well in life. On the surface, I appeared to be a semiengaged student taking notes as my teachers droned on and on about subjects I felt were irrelevant to my future. My lackluster GPA in high school reflected the amount of time I spent writing notes to my friends. Every time I had a classroom management issue as a teacher, I accepted it as a karmic payback for the rude behavior of my young student self. Had cell phones existed then, I would have been a texting madwoman. When I would confess this to my colleagues, they would scoff and make claims about how "these kids today" are different. After a while I started ignoring the girl texting in the back of the class, smiling as she looked down at her phone under the desk. I kept my sarcastic comments to myself, and I spent less time issuing empty threats about cell phone use in my course policies. I started to understand texting as today's note writing.

Years passed and cameras emerged as a feature of the ever-present phone on my students' desks. Slowly, users started to understand how to control their phones, and the jukebox of ring tones mercifully subsided. It was not until a group of students raised their cell phones to take a photo of my notes on the whiteboard that I started to rethink the possibilities. I stood there awkwardly as my students took a photo of my half-baked scrawling. One student texted the photo to one student who was absent, while another e-mailed the photo to her presentation group. Hours later, I got e-mails from students wanting to follow up with questions about the photographed lecture notes. Right before my eyes, my students taught me a new way to see the cell phone—as a potential learning tool.

Weeks later, the same group of students started their presentations with a cell phone poll. "Okay, everyone," one student said. "Here's something you'll never hear a teacher say: 'Take out your cell phone!'" Everyone laughed at her obvious dig at teachers as I attempted to conceal my tragically uncool and dated flip phone. My old-timey "handset" quickly became a source of amusement for a group of students in the front row. For many of my students, seeing a flip phone was a walk down memory lane, as they had quickly cycled through this cell phone build version sometime in middle school. *Call of Duty* meets *Pong*, I thought to myself.

By the time I figured out the directions, most students had taken out their smartphones and participated in the poll. Every single person participated in the poll, and the group used the real-time data to transition to their next point. One student did not have a phone and her neighbor offered to text her response. For about three minutes there was total chaos in the room, but as soon as the group started with their presentation, the class got quiet. I watched in astonishment as all of the students in the audience put away their phones and listened to the presentation. The real-time bar graph generated by the poll got their attention as an audience, and the group then strategically referred to the poll responses throughout the presentation. Student engagement was focused and sustained. It was one of the best student presentations I had seen, and subsequent group presentations also incorporated cell phone polls.

The next day I asked the students why they put their phones away once the poll was over. Surely they could have checked their e-mail or taken a quick scroll through social media. They looked at me like I was insane. One student, with that look of pity people get when they have to explain something obvi-ous, said, "Um, because we didn't need them anymore." Some students' laugh-ter insinuated that I was losing credibility as the most learned person in the room. I am pretty sure that if I had not already established a positive rapport with these students, I would have heard a few "duh, Ms. Indrunas" snickers around the room. I was so fascinated by their use of cell phones, I asked the group to share with me how they learned about cell phone polls. Little did I know I was opening a crack in the dam of student frustration; my lesson plan that day got completely derailed.

Hands went up when I asked if they used cell phone polls or iClickers[1] in other classes. They explained to me that they tried to learn about cell phone polls in order to find an alternative to what they saw as the ridiculously expen-sive iClickers. According to them, one teacher made them buy iClickers that they used only once during an entire quarter. "I paid 45 bucks for this use-less thing, so I wanted to show the teacher that she could use something else for free," she explained, "but she claimed she'd put so much time into using iClickers that she was going to stick with them." Her friend shook her head and asked, "Why do teachers make us buy stuff that we won't use again?" Another student suggested that maybe she should start a fashion trend by making her iClicker into a set of earrings as she held them up to her ears. I laughed with them at the time, but my mood soured as I pondered this new learning technology that was then being advertised as a slam-dunk solu-tion for student engagement. As I tried to empathize, I remembered that I am still paying interest on textbooks that were "required" for courses but that my undergraduate teachers never assigned readings from or referenced in any way during class. My students' frustration about these iClickers resonated with me. At least my books eventually decorated my personal home library, but these semidisposable devices were on their way to the landfill.

As a faculty member, I felt guilty for not using iClickers, but then again, I had not been impressed with the training that had been offered. I will admit that I enjoy learning about technology, but when I attended the iClicker train-ing, I left thinking they were not a good fit for my discipline. As a writing teacher, I had very little use for multiple-choice quizzes, which seemed to be the emphasis of the training.

When I examined the company's training materials on my own, I quickly grew frustrated by all of the steps involved in using the device. The process seemed excessively time consuming given the potential return on investment. I had also been in a workshop with a fellow teacher who spent hours setting up questions that did not work when she got to class. The teacher reported that she looked like a fool in front of her students, and she ultimately felt that it would have saved her time just to stick with the decidedly analog note-card method she had been using in her assessments for decades. The more technologically savvy teachers spoke of their increased student engagement and increased test scores as a result of the iClicker. They loved them! The other teachers, though, for whom the rapid advances in technology presented an unpleasant challenge, sat there in silence. Combined with my students' perspectives, these peer concerns clearly identified a problem. Students were spending an incredible amount of money on technology that most teachers struggled to effectively implement.

As I made the transition into a new career helping teachers learn about educational technology, I wanted to address the growing digital divide between teachers who struggled with technology and those for whom it came easily. In my earlier work as an adjunct instructor, I had recognized online teaching as a burgeoning opportunity at a time when tenured and tenure-track faculty seemed largely uninterested. Learning about technology was rewarding to me, and I saw it as a skill that would help my career. I also sympathized with colleagues who spent countless unpaid hours trying to stay current in their understanding and implementation of new learning technologies. The iClicker can be an amazing tool for teachers who are comfortable with such specialized technologies. For teachers at the other end of the spectrum, iClickers are cumbersome, frustrating, and time consuming to learn. Cell phone polls, however, can be a gateway technology for teachers struggling to use 21st-century tools. The ease with which this readily available technology can be used to collect real-time data empowers teachers and students to collaboratively explore new applications for networked educational technologies.

Angel Brady (2012) has taken a similar view. She noted,

> Clickers are a great tool to help you engage your students, receive instant feedback from your students about understanding concepts you are teaching, and to get an overall feel for your student audience. The one hurdle that is attached to the physical Clicker technology is all the bulky hardware. Clickers involve setting a receiver, setting the code for the physical instructor clicker with the software, and making sure each student has a workable physical Clicker.

Brady's post went on to explore other ways teachers can use this type of technology in ways that are free to both teachers and students. In regard to the desirability of instant (and comfortably anonymous) data, her post substantiated what I was learning in my own experience with teachers. However, her reservations about the hardware that makes such data available led me to consider the alternatives. Indeed, cell phone polls are more readily available, are not an additional financial burden to students, and are easier to learn and implement than iClickers.

When I transitioned from teaching into administrative work, my first job as an instructional designer was to assist the college's Fire Science faculty in adapting their face-to-face courses to an online learning environment. This retraining was mandatory, and tensions were sometimes high among faculty who did not wish to teach online at all. In short, this was a cohort who did not see themselves as computer savvy. When I sent out a preassessment survey, I received a surprising number of negative responses. For the faculty, this was their first chance to vent about a transition they thought had been decided by administrative fiat, and they made it clear that this was not a direction for their department that they supported. They not only doubted the usefulness of the technology, but also resented that the college was "forcing" them out of their preferred teaching environment. On my very first day with them, they echoed these sentiments with their arms emphatically crossed. Frowns formed under their mustaches as I began my presentation. I did notice, however, that they all had iPhones and iPads next to their paper notepads. When I asked about their use of social media, every single one of them reported being on Facebook. They even admitted to enjoying the online trainings they did for their jobs. As I listened to them, I decided to try a cell phone poll for the very first time with a live audience of teachers. Having participated in my students' group presentation polls, I felt confident that I could do it too. With my students I had embraced a moment of participatory chaos as everybody scrambled to input their responses on their phones, and I was curious to see how a room full of teachers would react.

Prior to this meeting, I created a cell phone poll with a few basic questions about their concerns regarding online teaching. Their contempt for and blatant doubt regarding educational technology pushed me to do something I'd never done in a faculty training session. I told them all to take out their cell phones, and once I explained the directions they quickly became immersed in the activity. As they texted their responses, we watched the bar graphs change as more people in the room understood how the process worked. They seemed to be enjoying themselves because their responses were anonymous. Having taught the basics of rhetorical appeal for almost a decade, I turned to pathos to convince them that online learning had potential. Having taught online myself, I told them, I worked with people in my courses that couldn't make it to campus for traditional classes for a variety of reasons. For example, I hypothesized that there is a grocery clerk who has to work to support his family, but who ultimately aspires to become a firefighter. All of us know somebody, I told them, who hates her job but can't find a way out; online classes help such people. Working myself into full evangelical mode about the future of online education, I shared with them my personal story and explained that had this type of learning opportunity existed when I was a student, I could have shortened my tenure as a cocktail waitress. Shoulders relaxed and arms uncrossed as everybody leaned forward to take notes. Smiles formed under mustaches, and from then on, the firefighters were simpatico. One of them asked if he could change his answers on the cell phone poll that we just did. In real time I watched their negative responses turn to optimistic ones, and I felt a measure of relief at the front of the room as I basked momentarily in the warm glow of a successful, and perhaps rare, group conversion among teachers.

We then had a robust conversation about the many specialized technologies in their field and how many times they had to attend trainings to update their skills. Without knowing this would happen, the cell phone poll exercise built up their confidence. One of them admitted that he thought online education was the future and that he was excited about it. Another agreed that this would help him relate to his son and his grandchildren. The cell phone poll, it turned out, was a tool they could use in their classrooms that week. The training session ended, and I had to leave for another appointment, but they all stayed a few minutes late, chatting excitedly with their program's administrative assistant. As I walked away, she shot me two thumbs up with a huge smile.

The next time I met with the firefighters, they told me how they had used cell phone polls in their class and that they also saw the potential for using them in the workplace. Firefighter instructors often teach in the field, so this "cell phone thing" that I taught them could be an effective part of such workplace lessons. Those in leadership positions shared that they liked the anonymity of the responses because it allowed them to weigh in as "just one of the guys" helping to give feedback instead of conspicuously speaking as "the boss." They liked the idea of senior staff pop-quizzing younger staff members about crucial protocols. Without really knowing I had had an agenda, I convinced a group of avowed skeptics to think of themselves as both adaptable and capable when it came to incorporating new learning technologies into their classes. One of them e-mailed me to let me know that this "tech stuff" was already helping him to revise and improve his face-to-face class.

From then on, I continued to advocate the use of cell phone polls in community college professional technical courses. Cell phone polls are free, easy to use, and empowering for faculty members who are generally apprehensive about using technology in the classroom. Cell phone polls increase student engagement and foster genuinely interactive, evidence-based discussion. They also enable the solicitation of student feedback in an accessible, democratic milieu that allows even the most introverted students to offer their views. For instance, during one of my training sessions about technology, one chemistry teacher asked, "Why don't we just raise our hands? That's easier, right?" Without missing a beat, an aviation instructor responded, "This will help me look cool with the younger students. I can see how this will help me win them over." Here I was, the supposed expert in the room, and his response had never crossed my mind. Yes, they can raise their hands, but cell phone polls allow students to use technology they love.

My experience as a faculty member and instructional designer for the Fire Science program helped me land a job as my college's director of eLearning. My first quarter was especially difficult because we were transitioning to a new learning management system, and faculty stress was running especially high. Without knowing it, I was leading a group of faculty who were experiencing learning management system "migration fatigue." One teacher took it upon herself to share her frustration about technology with her department peers, the division dean, the vice president, and anyone who would listen. That week I was questioning my sanity for beginning a new job at the same time that a campus-wide learning management system transition was underway. The Cosmetology Department had booked me to train them and answer their questions. I drove out to a satellite campus building with a sense of dread; I was growing frustrated by faculty complaints about something I could not control. To my surprise, what I found was a delightful group of teachers who were ready to make changes within their department. They wanted to use iPads instead of bulky paper binders to store and review hairstyle and makeup-application examples, and they had heard about my cell phone poll training from some of their Fire Science acquaintances. As we sat in the instructors' office meeting area, they took out their cell phones and I demonstrated how the polling process works. They texted their responses and watched the bar graph change on the computer screen at the front of the room. Shortly thereafter, they were discussing their findings and talking about ways they could use the polls in their classrooms.

Minutes later I was completely lost as they began to employ the specialized terminology of their discourse community, but what I observed was how empowered they were as I taught one of them to create a multiple-choice poll. She looked at me incredulously and said, "That's it? That's so cool!" These working professionals and fellow teachers quickly recognized that an existing and easily overlooked technology could be recontextualized to suit their pedagogical aims. They quickly began to improvise and innovate. The next day one of the teachers e-mailed me to let me know that her students loved using their cell phones and that they had gone from apathetic note takers to "beyond engaged." One of the students asked her if they were going to do a poll tomorrow. "Students wanted to be quizzed," she mused. "Can you believe it?" A few months later I asked the same cosmetology teacher to do a presentation and to describe her new practices. One teacher in attendance remarked in an anonymous survey that he needed to "up [his] game because the Cosmetology teachers were making [him] look bad."

These experiences with teachers in my college's professional technical programs proved the viability of integrating gateway technologies into other modalities of classroom instruction. The advantages are many, and the ease with which teachers can learn the technology convinces them to take risks on their own. Having been a faculty member who discovered the potential advantages of teaching with as-yet-unproven technologies, I have learned that not all faculty members are eager to take risks with unknown methods and that some may feel that their particular disciplines do not readily allow for such experimentation. In my own teaching career, I benefited from considerable departmental autonomy, and I was free to adopt and discard different classroom technologies as experience dictated. I could often turn a lesson that had fizzled into a teachable moment by showing my students that I also benefited from a process of reflection and revision. I realize that in some disciplines teachers feel that their methodologies are necessarily constrained by calls for efficiency and timeliness of goals met, but I believe that the adoption of a demonstrably effective classroom activity—utilizing a familiar technology that is already at hand—will prove to such teachers to be a worthwhile addition to their pedagogical repertoire.

NOTE

1. The iClicker, also stylized as "i>clicker," is a brand-name classroom response system (CRS) that includes hardware (transmitters and receivers) and software, although the term *iClicker* is sometimes applied generically to any CRS using dedicated devices, as opposed to systems that use existing technology such as cell phones or Internet-based polling. At the time of this writing, students pay $45 to $55 for a hand-held transmitter (clicker).

REFERENCE

Brady, A. (2012). Alternatives to physical clickers in the classroom [Blog post]. Educational Technologies Blog, Princeton University. Retrieved December 15, 2014, from http://blogs.princeton.edu/etc/2012/04/10/alternatives-to-physical-clickers-in-the-classroom

Appendix: Further Resources

Peter D. Wallis

COMPREHENSIVE RESOURCE WEBSITES

Carl Wieman Science Education Initiative (2014). Clicker resources. The University of British Columbia. Retrieved November 6, 2014, from http://www.cwsei.ubc.ca/resources/clickers.htm
The Carl Wieman Science Education Initiative, working with both the University of Colorado–Boulder and the University of British Columbia, has put together one of the most complete online resource sets for clicker use. Resources include guides, videos of advanced and basic practice, sample questions, and group work best practices.

Bruff et al. (2014). Classroom response systems ("clickers"). Vanderbilt University. Retrieved November 6, 2014, from http://cft.vanderbilt.edu/guides-sub-pages/clickers/
In addition to providing support for the Vanderbilt community, this Center for Teaching page provides a helpful quick overview of terminology, definitions, example question types, and activity suggestions. Bruff also includes a very helpful classroom response system bibliography (http://cft.vanderbilt.edu/docs/classroom-response-system-clickers-bibliography/).

Center for New Designs in Learning and Scholarship (2014). Clickers community of practice. Georgetown University. Retrieved November 6, 2014, from https://blogs.commons.georgetown.edu/clickers_cop/
Although limited, this site demonstrates a strong community of practice infrastructure for clickers and hosts a number of resources available to everyone. These include articles of interest and very brief and practical faculty stories of clicker use.

QUICK OVERVIEWS

Duncan, D. (2008). Tips for successful "clicker" use. University of Colorado. Retrieved November 6, 2014, from http://casa.colorado.edu/~dduncan/clickers/Tips.pdf

Written from a STEM practitioners' perspective, Douglas Duncan's recommendations include Carl Wieman Science Education Initiative recommendations. This two-page document functions as the quickest and most accessible "checklist" for instructors new to clickers.

EDUCAUSE Learning Initiative (2005). *Seven things you should know about clickers.* Retrieved November 6, 2014, from http://www.educause.edu/taxonomy/term/28524
One of the best resources for quick answers to "Who, what, where, why, when?" questions about classroom response, written at a high level. Educause and ELI's publications tend to be very practitioner focused, if light on citations.

Crews, T. B., Ducate, L., Rathel, J. M., Heid, K., & Bishoff, S. T. (2011). *Clickers in the classroom: Transforming students into active learners.* (Research Bulletin 9, 2011). Boulder, CO: EDUCAUSE Center for Applied Research. Retrieved November 6, 2014, from http://www.educause.edu/ecar
This report gives a relatively quick, high-level overview of the reasons for and primary uses of clickers. Focused on the basic approach for the novice, the report would be especially useful for anyone seeking a broad and practical (and undetailed) outline of clicker use.

Keller, C., Finkelstein, N., Perkins, K., Pollock, S., Turpen, C., & Dubson, M. (2007). Research-based practices for effective clicker use. *2007 Physics Education Research Conference, 951*, 128–131. Retrieved November 6, 2014, from http://www.colorado.edu/physics/EducationIssues/papers/Turpen_etal/Effective_Clicker_Use.pdf
This short, four-page conference presentation gives an overview of clicker usage across (mainly STEM) departments at the University of Colorado–Boulder. Results of the study were analyzed to elucidate the relationships between most-used question types and statistical relationships between student feedback and instructor practices with clickers.

The McGraw Center for Teaching and Learning (2012). Alternatives to physical clickers in the classroom. Princeton University. Retrieved November 6, 2014, from http://blogs.princeton.edu/etc/2012/04/10/alternatives-to-physical-clickers-in-the-classroom/
Clickers are not the only way to gather feedback and engage in peer instruction. This brief blog article addresses an important issue: what to do when clickers, for whatever reason, are not the best choice.

LITERATURE REVIEWS

Caldwell, J. E. (2007). Clickers in the large classroom: Current research and best-practice tips. *CBE-Life Sciences Education, 6*(1), 9–20. (http://www.ncbi.nlm.nih.gov/pmc/articles/PMC1810212/)

While focused on the life sciences, Caldwell's literature review is broadly useful as an academic discussion of the general principles and practices in clicker use. The structure is easy to follow, and the general observations make the article a current, broad, and cohesive single account of using clickers in the classroom.

Fies, C., & Marshall, J. (2006). Classroom response systems: A review of the literature. *Journal of Science Education and Technology, 15*(1), 101–109.
Primarily for those interested in research on classroom response systems, this article focuses mainly on the methodologies used in clicker research. At the same time, lessons, especially pedagogical lessons, can easily be drawn from the authors' discussion of these topics. It is great reading for anyone interested in doing their own classroom response research.

Lantz, M. E. (2010). The use of "clickers" in the classroom: Teaching innovation or merely an amusing novelty? *Computers in Human Behavior, 26*(4), 556–561.
In one of the most recent literature reviews on clickers in the classroom, Lantz focuses on the ways clickers work, through active learning and enhanced student processing. The article will be interesting to anyone who wants to understand the underlying processes through which clickers can be effective.

Kay, R. H., & LeSage, A. (2009). Examining the benefits and challenges of using audience response systems: A review of the literature. *Computers & Education, 53*(3), 819–827.
Kay and LeSage's must-read article is a major review of the literature in this area. The article looks at the history of the technology and the terms used to describe it, followed by an in-depth review of 67 peer-reviewed papers published from 2000 to 2007. Kay and LeSage's article is particularly useful as a "map" of the work done so far, and where various techniques have been referenced and used in the past. Their literature review makes it easy to find articles that explore particular techniques and uses of classroom response systems.

BOOKS

Banks, D. A. (Ed.). (2006). *Audience response systems in higher education: Applications and cases.* Hershey, PA: Information Science Publishing.
An extensive discussion of both the history and cases of classroom/audience response education. Banks's volume is relatively comprehensive and will be helpful for anyone looking for in-depth history or specific cases within a broad variety of applications.

Bruff, D. (2009). *Teaching with classroom response systems: Creating active learning environments.* San Francisco, CA: Jossey-Bass.
This book focuses on the pedagogical practices in clicker use, incorporating case studies from a variety of disciplines, with a STEM focus. However, particularly helpful

chapters cover challenges both in the teaching and the technology and approach the taxonomy of clicker questions.

Duncan, D. (2005). *Clickers in the classroom: How to enhance science teaching using classroom response systems.* San Francisco, CA: Pearson Education.
This brief book provides a general, STEM-focused overview of clickers, from a basic-practitioner perspective.

HUMANITIES AND SOCIAL SCIENCES

Classroom response use and effectiveness in STEM fields is fairly well documented and can obscure the relatively few classroom response articles in the humanities and social sciences. Many STEM articles appear in the references to this book's individual chapters and in the literature reviews. Consequently, we've included a few key resources on the humanities and social sciences here.

Cole, S., & Kosc, G. (2010). Quit surfing and start "clicking": One professor's effort to combat the problems of teaching the US survey in a large lecture hall. *History Teacher, 43*(3), 397–410.
Immerwahr, J. (2009). Engaging the "thumb generation" with clickers. *Teaching Philosophy, 32*(3), 233–245.
Jenkins, A. (2007). Technique and technology: Electronic voting systems in an English literature lecture. *Pedagogy, 7*(3), 526–533.
Stuart, S. A., Brown, M. I., & Draper, S. W. (2004). Using an electronic voting system in logic lectures: One practitioner's application. *Journal of Computer Assisted Learning, 20*(2), 95–102.
Mollborn, S., & Hoekstra, A. (2010). "A Meeting of Minds": Using Clickers for Critical Thinking and Discussion in Large Sociology Classes. *Teaching Sociology, 38*(1), 18–27.
Schell, J. (2013). 3 easy ways to use clickers and peer instruction in the arts and humanities. Turn to Your Neighbor: The Official Peer Instruction Blog. Retrieved November 6, 2014, from http://blog.peerinstruction.net/2013/06/10/3-easy-ways-to-use-clickers-and-peer-instruction-in-the-arts-and-humanities/

HOW CLICKERS CHANGE TEACHER PRACTICE

Kolikant, Y. B. D., Drane, D., & Calkins, S. (2010). "Clickers" as catalysts for transformation of teachers. *College Teaching, 58*(4), 127–135.

QUESTION/CONCEPTEST BANKS

Project Galileo. Retrieved November 6, 2014, from https://galileo.seas.harvard.edu/login/

MathQUEST/MathVote. Retrieved November 6, 2014, from http://mathquest.carroll.edu/

Physics from University of Colorado Boulder. Retrieved November 6, 2014, from http://www.colorado.edu/physics/EducationIssues/cts/

Statistics from University of Oklahoma. Retrieved November 6, 2014, from http://www.ou.edu/statsclickers/clickerQuestions.htm

Statistics from Simon Fraiser University. Retrieved November 6, 2014, from http://people.stat.sfu.ca/~cschwarz/quest.html

ConcepTests for chemistry from Chemistry Exchange. Retrieved November 6, 2014, from http://www.jce.divched.org/JCEDLib/QBank/collection/ConcepTests/

ConcepTests for chemistry from Brandeis. Retrieved November 6, 2014, from http://people.brandeis.edu/~herzfeld/conceptests.html

Many more resources are available, and in many cases their effectiveness will depend upon the systems you are using. Most response system vendors have a knowledge base already constructed, and many of them have produced videos and tutorials on how to use their systems. We recommend that you ask questions on your own and do research on the ecosystem surrounding your own use of classroom response.

About the Editors and Contributors

EDITORS

David S. Goldstein teaches American and ethnic studies in the School of Interdisciplinary Arts and Sciences at the University of Washington Bothell, where he also serves as director of the Teaching and Learning Center. He earned a PhD in comparative culture at the University of California–Irvine and publishes on ethnic American literature and on the scholarship of teaching and learning. He is the coeditor of *Complicating Constructions: Race, Ethnicity and Hybridity in American Texts* (University of Washington Press, 2007).

Peter D. Wallis supports teaching and learning with all kinds of technologies at the University of Washington. He is an instructional technologist with UW-IT and a doctoral student in the UW College of Education, where he recently earned his MEd. He is engaged in research in teaching and learning with technology, in the neuroscience of education, and the day-to-day practice of learning technologies. He tries to make time for poetry, fiction, and Western martial arts, and lives where he can watch the boats with Grace.

CONTRIBUTORS

Traci Freeman is the director of the Colket Center for Academic Excellence at Colorado College, where she oversees student academic support, contributes to faculty development, and teaches courses in the Department of Education. She has a PhD in English from the University of Texas at Austin. Her research focuses on writing pedagogy, writing center and academic support center administration, and noncognitive factors that affect student learning and success in college.

Robyn E. Goacher is an assistant professor of chemistry in the College of Arts and Sciences at Niagara University, where she teaches courses in instrumental analysis and analytical, environmental, and inorganic chemistry. Dr. Goacher earned her PhD in chemistry at SUNY–Buffalo, where she specialized in surface analysis and depth profiling of semiconductors. She has published articles about the surface analysis of semiconductor and biological materials, with a current research focus on analytical methods for detection of enzyme activity on wood. Dr. Goacher enjoys the challenge of developing an interesting and impactful chemistry curriculum for undergraduates and of developing herself as a scholar of teaching and learning.

Alison J. Green is an assistant professor at the William F. Harrah College of Hotel Administration at the University of Nevada, Las Vegas. Green earned her PhD from the University of New Mexico in organizational learning and instructional technology, and she is a passionate teacher and researcher as well as the cofounder of the hospitality learners model, which investigates learning theory in hospitality education. She embraces life by injecting creativity and innovation into both teaching and research, with the end goal of heightening student engagement.

Alyson Indrunas is the director of eLearning and Instructional Design at Everett Community College. She holds an MA in English studies from Western Washington University and an MEd in continuing and college education from the Woodring College of Education. Her scholarly interests are in educational technology, professional development, open educational resources, and instructional design. She is the cochair of the EvCC Textbook Alternative Committee, which supports faculty adoption of open educational resources. She hopes her career transition from English adjunct to eLearning, which was featured in *Vitae*, inspires other contingent faculty. She lives in Bellingham, Washington.

Ron Krabill teaches cultural studies, media studies, and African studies in the School of Interdisciplinary Arts and Sciences at the University of Washington Bothell, where he directs the MA in Cultural Studies program. He holds a PhD in sociology and historical studies from the New School for Social Research and serves on the executive board of the Simpson Center for the Humanities. His research focuses on media and politics in South Africa, discourses of global citizenship, and critical community-based pedagogy. He is the author of *Starring Mandela and Cosby: Media and the End(s) of Apartheid* (Chicago, 2010).

Danyelle Moore is currently the instructional support specialist at Niagara University, where she assists faculty with professional development through workshops and individual consultations focusing on instructional technology and course development. She uses her education and business background to support the online initiatives at the university. Ms. Moore earned her BS in business education and her MS in special education from Niagara University. She has published on the topics of effective technology use in the classroom and the scholarship of teaching and learning (SoTL).

Ashley Harris Paul teaches English at Bunker Hill Community College in Boston, Massachusetts. Prior to that, she was a communications learning specialist in the Learning Commons at Tallahassee Community College in Tallahassee, Florida, where she worked with students one-on-one and participated in the training of tutors. Ms. Paul earned an MFA with a concentration in fiction from Florida State University, and she has published her work in *Pembroke Magazine*, *Apalachee Review*, and *Southeast Review*, among others. She currently lives in Malden, Massachusetts, with her husband, son, and Boston terrier.

Luis Sanchez teaches organic chemistry in the College of Arts and Sciences at Niagara University. He received his PhD in organic chemistry from Michigan State University and has worked on synthetic/medicinal research both in industrial and academic settings. Dr. Sanchez appreciates that, as a professor, he can unleash his passion for molecules while taking part in the great challenge of guiding future generations of scientists in these changing times. Besides doing research and teaching, Dr. Sanchez enjoys traveling, running long distances, and going to theater plays.

Paul R. Schupp is an associate professor and chairs the Department of Criminology and Criminal Justice at Niagara University, where he teaches graduate and undergraduate courses on the principles of criminal justice, imprisonment and corrections, and corporate crime. He earned his PhD in criminology and criminal justice at SUNY–Albany and is a graduate of Cornell University. His primary scholarly interests are in critical criminology, the political economy of imprisonment, and elite deviance.

Yonghong Tong is an assistant professor of computer and information sciences in the College of Arts and Sciences at Niagara University. He obtained his PhD from the University of North Carolina–Charlotte in 2013. Dr. Tong's research centers on mobile and Web applications, information technology use in education, and data visualization. Dr. Tong is currently supervising student research in his areas of focus.

Brian Vanden Heuvel teaches botany and plant science in the Department of Biology at Colorado State University–Pueblo, where he is also the chair. He earned a PhD in botany from the University of Texas as Austin, and publishes on human pharmaceutical uptake into plants, phylogenetics, and plant diversity. He lives in Colorado Springs, Colorado, with a spouse, two children, and two cats.

Christopher H. Wade is an assistant professor at the University of Washington Bothell in the School of Nursing and Health Studies. He received his BA and PhD from Wesleyan University, and later an MPH from Johns Hopkins University. Dr. Wade's research uses his knowledge of genomics, health behavior, and social science research methods to explore the social and ethical implications of applied genetic technologies. A major focus of his teaching involves working with nursing and public health students to develop a critical appreciation for the methodological foundations of health research.

Paul S. Weiss is a senior associate at the Rollins School of Public Health at Emory University in Atlanta, Georgia. He teaches courses in basic biostatistical methods, complex sample designs, and statistical computing. He collaborates on a wide range of projects involving numerous aspects of public health and has worked with researchers around the world to improve quality of life for the global community. He lives in Lawrenceville, Georgia, with his wife and two children.

Index

management system. While the phrase "just in time" may evoke shades of slap-dash work and cut corners, JiTT pedagogy is just the opposite. It helps students view learning as a process that takes time, introspection, and persistence.

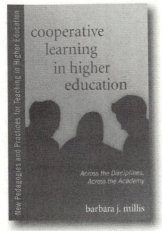

Cooperative Learning in Higher Education
Across the Disciplines, Across the Academy
Edited by Barbara J. Millis

Research has identified cooperative learning as one of the 10 high-impact practices that improve student learning.

If you've been interested in cooperative learning, but wondered how it would work in your discipline, this book provides the necessary theory, and a wide range of concrete examples.

The chapters showcase cooperative learning in action, at the same time introducing the reader to major principles such as individual accountability, positive interdependence, heterogeneous teams, group processing, and social or leadership skills.

Using Reflection and Metacognition to Improve Student Learning
Across the Disciplines, Across the Academy
Edited by Matthew Kaplan, Naomi Silver, Danielle LaVaque-Manty, and Deborah Meizlish
Foreword by James Rhem

Research has identified the importance of helping students develop the ability to monitor their own comprehension and to make their thinking processes explicit, and indeed demonstrates that metacognitive teaching strategies greatly improve student engagement with course material. This book—by presenting principles that teachers in higher education can put into practice in their own classrooms—explains how to lay the ground for this engagement, and help students become self-regulated learners actively employing metacognitive and reflective strategies in their education.

Sty/us

22883 Quicksilver Drive
Sterling, VA 20166-2102

Subscribe to our e-mail alerts: www.Styluspub.com

Also in the New Pedagogies and Practices for Teaching in Higher Education series:

Each volume of the series presents a specific pedagogy. The editors and contributors introduce the reader to the underlying theory and methodology; provide specific guidance in applying the pedagogy; and offer case studies of practice across a several disciplines, usually across the domains of the sciences, humanities, and social studies, and, if appropriate, professional studies.

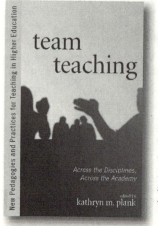

Team Teaching
Across the Disciplines, Across the Academy
Edited by Kathryn M. Plank

For those considering adopting team teaching, or interested in reviewing their own practice, this book offers an overview of this pedagogy, its challenges and rewards, and a rich range of examples in which teachers present and reflect upon their approaches.

This book provides insight into the impact of team teaching on student learning and on faculty development. It also addresses the challenges, both pedagogical and administrative, that need to be addressed for team teaching to be effective.

Just-in-Time Teaching
Across the Disciplines, Across the Academy
Edited by Scott Simkins and Mark H. Maier

"*Just-in-Time Teaching* commendably promotes the pedagogical procedure that bears its name (JiTT). The book is an excellent resource for professors who are serious pursuers of improving students' learning. . . . The text is adeptly compiled and skillfully written."

—*Teaching Theology and Religion*

"I found the ideas presented by the authors intriguing, and I'm already thinking about how I'm going to make use of them myself."

— *EDC Resource Review*

Just-in-Time Teaching (JiTT) is a pedagogical approach that requires students to answer questions related to an upcoming class a few hours beforehand, using an online course

(Continues on preceding page)